Kristen's Raw

The Easy Way to Get Started
& Succeed at the
Raw Food Vegan Diet & Lifestyle

by Kristen Suzanne

*Green
Butterfly
Press*

Scottsdale, Arizona

OTHER BOOKS BY KRISTEN SUZANNE

- *Kristen Suzanne's EASY Raw Vegan Entrees*
- *Kristen Suzanne's EASY Raw Vegan Desserts*
- *Kristen Suzanne's EASY Raw Vegan Soups*
- *Kristen Suzanne's EASY Raw Vegan Salads & Dressings*
- *Kristen Suzanne's EASY Raw Vegan Sides & Snacks*
- *Kristen Suzanne's EASY Raw Vegan Smoothies, Juices, Elixirs & Drinks (includes wine drinks!)*
- *Kristen Suzanne's EASY Raw Vegan Holidays*
- *Kristen Suzanne's EASY Raw Vegan Dehydrating*
- *Kristen Suzanne's Ultimate Raw Vegan Hemp Recipes*

COMING SOON

- *Kristen Suzanne's Raw Vegan Diet for EASY Weight Loss*
- *Kristen Suzanne's Ultimate Raw Vegan Chocolate Recipes*

For details, Raw Food resources, and Kristen's free Raw Food newsletter, please visit:

KristensRaw.com

For information on excerpting, reprinting or licensing portions of this book, please write to info@greenbutterflypress.com.

Green Butterfly Press
19550 N. Gray Hawk Drive, Suite 1042
Scottsdale, AZ 85255 USA

Library of Congress Control Number: 2008940014
Library of Congress Subject Heading:
1. Cookery (Natural foods) 2. Raw foods

ISBN: 978-0-9817556-0-1

1.3

CONTENTS

1. WHY RAW? 1

2. THE HEALTH LANDSCAPE TODAY 15

3. HOW RAW WORKS 29

4. ORGANICS 41

5. EXPECTATIONS 45

6. EXERCISE & PHYSICAL FITNESS 59

7. RAW QUESTIONS 67

8. CRAVINGS 85

9. SETTING YOURSELF UP TO WIN 89

10. MORE SURE-FIRE WAYS TO SUCCEED 109

11. GET FAMILY SUPPORT 127

12. A DAY IN THE LIFE OF RAW 135

13. GETTING STARTED 139

14. WHERE ARE YOU TODAY? 167

15. TRAVEL IN THE RAW 171

16. 14-DAY SAMPLE MEAL PLAN 181

17. RAW FOR INTERMEDIATES 191

18. SPROUTING 197

19. WORDS TO INSPIRE 201

CHAPTER 1

WHY RAW?

You know you should eat healthier, or you wouldn't have bought this book. So, congratulations, because you've already started down the road of success. But, knowing and doing are not the same thing. Knowledge alone is not going to make you a success. Action is the answer. Action is the power you need. Action gives you the results. As a beginner with Raw food, you have momentum on your side. You have the excitement of doing something new for yourself, and anything new is always interesting and fun, right? The trick is sticking to it. And, it takes a proven, sure-fire plan to succeed. That is what you have right here.

We've all heard time and again that we should eat more fruits and vegetables. The difference between that statement in the past versus today is that we now have exciting, delicious, and innovative ways to prepare whole fruits and vegetables as evidenced by the popularity of "Raw food," emerging as a new cuisine all its own. "Raw" no longer means boring salads and fruit plates. With Raw food cuisine, your world has now opened up to experiencing fresh whole fruits and vegetables like you never imagined they could be... *incredible!*

Eating more Raw food is one of the most amazing things you can do for yourself. If you're looking to experience life at its fullest, then you definitely need to start incorporating more Raw food into your daily food choices. If you're looking to be the happiest you've ever been, then this is the answer. The Raw Lifestyle is, hands down, the easiest way to help lose unwanted weight, eliminate or reduce cellulite, improve digestion, experience restful sleep, gain incredible amounts of energy, have brighter eyes, radiate with beautiful, glowing, and younger looking skin, experience mental clarity and energy like never before, and have a new lease on life... literally, including the prevention and even reversal of many diseases. Consider yourself lucky to start where you are right now. Not a day, month or year later. Because as every day, month and year passes, you'll look back with pride and enormous gratitude at having started when you did... today. To begin, you must have the mindset that you won't settle for anything less than your best self. Raise your standards because *you are worth it*. Are you ready for your new lease on life? Then, let's get started. Come into the world of Raw with me, and experience for yourself the most amazing health ever.

> *"Knowing is not enough; we must apply.*
> *Willing is not enough; we must do."*
>
> — Goethe

WHAT DOES "RAW" MEAN? SOME BASIC TERMINOLOGY

In today's culinary vernacular, the term "Raw food," (with a capital 'R') refers to 100% plant-based food that has never been heated above 115-118 degrees. Sometimes you'll hear the term "Raw" used interchangeably with "Living." There is a small difference. "Living foods," such as fresh fruit, are in a living state, where the enzymes are active and available. "Raw" can refer to foods that do not readily have their enzymes available, even though they have not been heated or destroyed. Nuts and seeds, for example, are considered "Raw" (if they have not been heat treated), but they are not "living" because they have enzyme inhibitors still intact. It's during the process of soaking that the

2

enzyme inhibitors are deactivated, converting them from merely Raw into Living food (more on that later).

WHY RAW?

There are so many reasons to eat Raw plant-based foods. My short answer to "Why Raw?" is simple and to the point: *Try it*. Just try it and see how you feel. It could change your life. It changed mine.

Why Raw? I'm asked this all the time. Or, maybe I should say that I'm often challenged with that question almost as if I have to defend my position. I think what really happens is that when people learn about Raw food, they suddenly realize they might be making the "wrong" choices with respect to their own food. And no one likes to admit they're wrong, especially not for something as fundamental, primal, and emotional as eating. It's like telling someone they don't know how to tie their shoes or they don't know how to raise their kids correctly. It's hard for people to acknowledge that *they* might actually be the reason they're not feeling well, or aging too fast, as a result of the food they put in their mouths. But, regardless of someone's age or what they have believed for years, it does not change one fundamental truth: We are all responsible for our own health. If you are not feeling well, or if you believe there might be more to this life, then perhaps it is time to try something new.

Living the Raw food lifestyle has made me a more effective person... in everything I do. I experience pure, sustainable energy all-day-long and I require less sleep. My body is in perfect shape and I gain strength and endurance in my exercise routine on a regular basis. Mentally, the benefits have blown me away. My focus is now clear and concentrated. My memory is tack-sharp (my measurement for this: I now use fewer post-it notes—haha!). My relationships are the best they've ever been, because I'm happy and I love myself. My once-debilitating headaches have ceased to exist. People all around me see the difference and comment on it—my skin glows with the radiance of brand new life, which is exactly how I feel. Raw is the best thing that has ever happened to me.

Whatever your passion is in life (family, business, exercise, meditation, hobbies, etc.), eating Raw will take it to unbelievable new heights. Raw food offers you the most amazing benefits—physically, mentally, and spiritually. It is *the* ideal choice for your food consumption to help you attain optimal health. Raw food is for people who want to live longer while feeling younger. It's for people who want to feel vibrant and alive, and want to enjoy life like never before.

"Nothing is worth more than this day."

— Goethe

THE MEANING OF HEALTH

If you want to know the meaning and value of health, just ask someone who *does not have it*. Take a walk around a hospital. Seriously. There is nothing like seeing the fear in someone's eyes, and in the eyes of those they love, to quickly snap you out of the delusion that health is to be taken for granted.

YOUR HEALTH: OWN IT!

Your health is your responsibility and no one else's. This is important. Your health is not your family's responsibility, or your doctor's, not the government's, and it's not a higher being's responsibility. It is yours. This might turn some people off, but it's true. The sooner you recognize it, the easier life is. Be empowered and own your health!

It was a revelation for me once I realized the impact I have on myself. I know the bottom line; I can control what I eat. I can't always control every other aspect of my life, such as traffic, weather, or job stress, but I can control what I eat. Interestingly, this (a healthy diet) actually makes dealing with all those other stresses in your life terrifically easier. I have seen people turn their lives around just by changing how and what they eat, and you can, too. As you become more mindful of what you put into your body, you immediately improve your life. The best part about it is that it's not something you have to "wait and see." You can literally start to feel the benefits within hours. You'll find that you don't have to "recover" after eating, like you used to when you ate heavy, bloating, cooked food. It is time to stop insulting your body, because you are all you have.

Keep this in mind... when someone becomes ill, it affects more than just that person. It affects the person's family and the people around them.

"What lies before us and what lies behind us is nothing compared to what lies within us."

— Ralph Waldo Emerson

THE FOOD HEALTH LADDER

Where Are You on the Lifestyle Ladder?

When thinking about our society's food choices, picture a ladder going from least healthy at the bottom to healthiest at the top (see "Food Health Ladder," next page). At the very bottom of the ladder is what most Americans eat every day:

1. The S.A.D. Diet – Grade: F

At the very bottom of the food ladder, you'll find the people who eat what is widely referred to as the "Standard American Diet"—appropriately referred to as S.A.D., because it is truly sad.

The SAD diet comprises animal and plant products, in particular, foods containing nutritionally deficient processed foods, high in sugars/starches, fats, cholesterol, chemicals and preservatives. Picture mid-America shoveling down sweetened cereals for breakfast, fast food for lunch, and hot dogs or pork chops for dinner, and you've got the picture. These people probably know they're eating crap, but their personal priorities do not place value on short- or long-term health.

2. The F.*.C.K.E.D. Diet – Grade: D

One step up from the S.A.D. diet is that which I've not so tongue-in-cheekly called the "Food Understanding Corrupted, Killing Even Doctors" diet.

This is the diet eaten by most Americans who think they are eating healthily: chicken instead of beef, grilled instead of fried, skim milk instead of 2%, whole grain bread instead of Wonder Bread. Does this sound like anyone you know?... it should; it describes the vast majority of anybody who tries at all to eat well in our society. Unfortunately, it's a totally false sense of security. In a way, this is the saddest diet of all, because most of these people really, truly, are trying to eat well, but they are lacking something fundamental: information... very important facts about what is healthy and what is not. But here is the problem: They receive information from the media and their doctors in terms of *relative health*—relative compared to the horribly disease-ridden S.A.D. baseline, not absolute terms about what is truly optimal for the human body based on *all available data*.

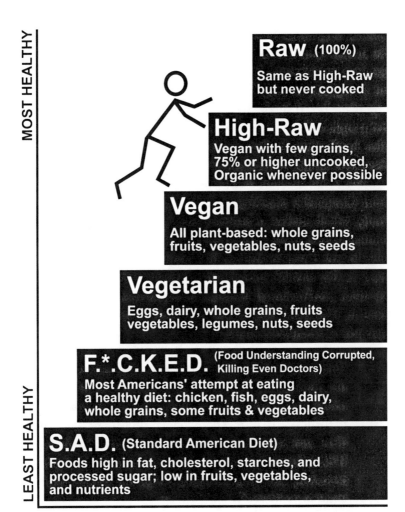

Raw (100%)
Same as High-Raw
but never cooked

High-Raw
Vegan with few grains,
75% or higher uncooked,
Organic whenever possible

Vegan
All plant-based: whole grains,
fruits, vegetables, nuts, seeds

Vegetarian
Eggs, dairy, whole grains, fruits
vegetables, legumes, nuts, seeds

F.*.C.K.E.D. (Food Understanding Corrupted,
Killing Even Doctors)
Most Americans' attempt at eating
a healthy diet: chicken, fish, eggs, dairy,
whole grains, some fruits & vegetables

S.A.D. (Standard American Diet)
Foods high in fat, cholesterol, starches, and
processed sugar; low in fruits, vegetables,
and nutrients

The Food Health Ladder

Most health studies conducted in the U.S. implicitly assume that Americans will never change their habits dramatically, so they don't even bother to look into things that sound extreme to the uninformed majority. Such is the case with Harvard's

7

famous, long-range Nurse's Health Study linking diet with things like breast cancer over the lifetime of those studied. With over 350,000 participants, it is one of the largest studies of its kind, but it neglects to even look at cases in which women consume only plant-based foods, based on the flawed circular reasoning that people will never eat that way because they don't today. The false implication is that a relatively high incidence of many diseases is simply unavoidable. This is good science at its worst!

For a full account of this problem, I highly recommend T. Colin Campbell's shocking and life-changing book, *The China Study*, which makes a brilliant case causally linking Western (animal-based) diets with Western diseases. This may not be news to you if you're reading this book, but what will make you angry is the media's reluctance to report Campbell's rigorous, repeated, peer-reviewed findings. Most doctors don't even know about it. Why don't they know? Get ready to be outraged... from page 287 of Campbell's book:

> *"Professor Willett and I have had discussions about the findings... I have always made the same point: whole foods, plant-based diets... are not included in the Nurses' Health Study cohort, and these types of diets are most beneficial to our health. Professor Willett has said to me, in response, on more than one occasion, 'You may be right, Colin, but people don't want to go there.'"*

Dr. Campbell continues,

> *"Scientists should not be ignoring ideas just because we perceive that the public does not want to hear them. Consumers have the ultimate choice of whether to integrate our findings into their lifestyles, but we [scientists] owe it to them to give them the*

best information possible with which to make that decision and not decide for them."

So while the typical gym-going, "heart-smart"-eating American thinks he or she is taking adequate control of his or her health, the truth is, the vast majority of their diets get a Grade D when compared to the range of *actual* dietary choices, as opposed to those imposed upon us by an entrenched system of habits, social norms, agricultural subsidies, biased policy-makers, and self-perpetuating ignorance.

3. The Vegetarian Diet – Grade: C

Vegetarians don't eat animal flesh (red meat, chicken, fish, etc.), but they do eat animal by-products, most notably, milk, cheese, and eggs.

Because milk, cheese, and eggs contain most of the same things that make meat unhealthy to eat, it cannot be considered a particularly healthy diet. In fact, I would advise people to cut out dairy and egg yolks even before meat!

4. The Vegan Diet – Grade: B

Next rung up the food health ladder is the vegan diet. Vegans don't consume any animal products or by-products (including honey in most cases). In fact, vegans typically don't wear or use leather either, depending on their personal reason for going vegan. If you eat a vegan diet for health and diet reasons, as opposed to ethical reasons, then it's possible that you'll consume honey and wear leather.

The leap from vegetarian to vegan is very significant—even bigger than the leap from meat-eating to vegetarianism—both in terms of health benefits and lifestyle impact. In fact, once you go vegan, you'll think that vegetarianism isn't really that different than eating meat... in fact, it's not that different, from both health and ethical perspectives (caged dairy cows don't fare any better than beef cows, and some would say the dairy cows suffer quite a bit more... before being slaughtered because they can no longer produce their quota of milk).

From a lifestyle perspective, veganism requires a bigger adjustment than vegetarianism because it's easy to order something without meat in most restaurants—and your server knows what meat looks like—whereas milk, eggs, and cheese are ingredients IN more dishes than you would have ever realized. Many servers, chefs, and restaurateurs still do not even know what vegan *IS*, let alone offer vegan options on the menu.

That said, it's worth it. Vegans who get a lot of fruits and vegetables in their diets (as opposed to "junk food vegans," who eat doughnuts, Oreos, Coke and fries for their meals) live longer, healthier, more vibrant lives than anybody on the planet. Going vegan is really the minimum place you want to be on the ladder if you are truly serious about taking control of your health and grading yourself against what is possible, rather than against a baseline of the masses that accepts disease as unavoidable and something to be treated after the fact with drugs.

Here are some startling statistics from John Robbins' best-selling book *The Food Revolution*:

- Average cholesterol level in the United States: 210
- Average cholesterol level of U.S. vegetarians: 161
- Average cholesterol level of U.S. vegans: 133

- Obesity rate among the general U.S. population: 18%
- Obesity rate among vegetarians: 6%
- Obesity rate among vegans: 2%

- Average weight of vegan adults compared to non-vegetarian adults: 10-20 pounds lighter

5. The High-Raw Diet – Grade: A

Next up on the ladder of food health are people who eat what's called a "High Raw" diet. It's 100% plant-based (organic when possible), and 75% (or more) food that is not heated above 115 degrees.

The leap from vegan to High Raw is pretty substantial, both in terms of health benefits and lifestyle impact, but it's made easy by two important things. First, High Raw's health impacts can be felt immediately. We're not talking about avoiding heart disease down the road (you probably already did that by going vegan); we're talking about energy, vitality, restful sleep, clear skin, good digestion, and so on... right away! It's very exciting. (Actually, in addition to the short-term benefits, Raw food's high concentration of phytonutrients and antioxidants is an excellent defense against cancer, and may be the single best reason for making the leap.)

Second, going vegan is like flipping a switch for most people, going all or none. Raw, on the other hand, is easily seen as a gradient. You can start eating 10% of your meals as Raw, and gradually work your way up... 25%, 50%, and so on.

In fact, it's this gradient aspect that necessitated the need for the term "High Raw," for all those people who eat "mostly Raw" but are not 100%. Most of the Raw fooders I know are High Raw, including myself. I might go a month or two being 100% Raw, but then go out to dinner and enjoy some cooked vegetables and tofu. I can usually feel the difference right away—a little sluggish, not quite as healthy—but food is more than just calories and nutrients. It's social. It's experiential. It's a source of pleasure and variety. I say, "all things in moderation." When you've made 100% Raw your "ideal," then you move your whole index. Suddenly, a steaming plate of cooked vegetables or a vegan chocolate chip cookie might be your occasional indulgence. Or a reward for something. Or a little sneaky cheating! I'm here to tell you that it's OKAY!

Think about it... your "cheating" is a thousand times healthier than all those poor F.*.C.K.E.D souls when they are on their *best* behavior!!

6. The 100% Raw Diet – Grade: A+

On the very top rung of the ladder, you'll see people who live the Raw lifestyle to the fullest in every way, because they're eating the healthiest cuisine in the world. With this lifestyle, it's all about plant-based foods, organic when possible and not heating food above 115 degrees.

Many, many people live a 100% Raw lifestyle. It is possible, it is fun, it is rewarding, and most of all, it is actually pretty easy once you get used to it! And by the time you finish this book, you'll know everything you need to know about adopting the lifestyle.

Remember, our digestive systems evolved in a world before we had acquired fire for cooking or weapons for hunting. When these innovations came along, they helped us survive by getting more food (in the form of meat) and killing potential parasites by cooking this relatively new thing called meat.

These innovations got us where we are today, both good and bad. The human race is populous, but sick. In Western society, we're no longer worried about starving, so we have the luxury of returning to our more healthful, ancestral dietary roots.

Going Raw, especially going 100% Raw, is not radical, it's not new. It is returning to our ancient true selves. It is eating the food that our bodies are designed to eat.

BABY STEPS

Everyone is at a different point on this ladder, and wherever you are today, you will probably look back at some point in the future to that spot as just a distant memory, because you'll be climbing higher and higher, while experiencing better and better health with each step up the ladder. For this reason, it does not matter where you are right now, the point is you have the power to change that.

Every little change you make for the better is going to help get you to the next higher step on the ladder, and that means improvement. That's awesome. In my opinion, there is no need to jump from the bottom to the top all at once. In fact, it's often difficult for people to do that. My goal is to support people on every step, be it a baby step or a big leap, as you move into healthier places and new times for your life. It does not matter where you are today, because by next week or next month or next year, you could be much higher as you make better choices for healthier living. For instance, if you're at the bottom and you remove, say, dairy from your diet, that's a huge step. You move higher on the ladder of health. Congratulations! Then, you remove meat and you move even higher, as you continue to experience greater health. Or, maybe you're a vegan and you eat a lot of flour-based, starchy foods. A step to improve could be to start eating more fresh vegetables and fruits. Or, maybe you're 50% Raw and you want to make your life 75% Raw.

The point is that you don't want to focus on the totality of the daunting mountain in front of you... just concentrate on the *next step* and taking it to higher health. That one step is the only thing that matters right now.

"Take the first step in faith. You don't have to see the whole staircase, just take the first step."

— Dr. Martin Luther King, Jr.

CHAPTER 2

THE HEALTH LANDSCAPE TODAY

The main health challenges with Americans today are diabetes, heart disease, cancer, obesity, osteoporosis, and depression. You won't find these same challenges in all parts of the world, but you will find them everyplace that eats the typical Western diet. Even more interesting, and tragic, is that these diseases are appearing in large numbers for the first time *ever* in cultures that are adopting the Western diet, in particular, animal-based foods.

If you take a look at the world's longest living cultures, you will find that they do not even have words in their vocabulary for some of the diseases we are afflicted with here in the United States. Hearth disease, cancer, diabetes, obesity, osteoporosis and depression are practically unknown in those parts of the world. We might as well refer to our American eating habit as "The Suicide Diet," because I heard somewhere (and I agree) that eating is the biggest cause of disability, disease, and death in the United States today.

I had an "a-ha" moment when I thought about the prospect of finding out someday that I could have cancer, heart disease or diabetes. After all, it's in my family. When I imagined I could end up going to the doctor and finding out this news someday, I realized that the doctor would give me a prescription or treatment for whatever was ailing me. This might seem fine for some people. But, what you might not recognize is that when you get a prescription or have a treatment for a disease such as heart disease, cancer, or diabetes, you find out that you will probably be taking the drugs for the *rest of your life*. Wow... think about that... You take it for the rest of your life! They don't cure the disease, they essentially make you dependent on an expensive subscription to manufactured chemicals. Although that makes the pharmaceutical companies happy, it certainly didn't make me happy to think about it. I don't ever want to take a medication for the rest of my life. I can only imagine the side effects and quality of life I'd have if I did.

According to Dr. Richard Brannon, chairman of the board of trustees for the International Academy of Preventative Medicine, "Most of the food in America today will support life, but it won't support health." I agree with this statement wholeheartedly. There is a difference between just living life, going through the motions, versus living life to the fullest and loving every day of it because you are truly healthy. I think a lot of people do not realize the potential health they could experience because they've never felt that way before. It goes along with the saying, "you don't know what you don't know."

There have been so many cases of people that have stopped, and even reversed, a number of conditions related to poor health by eating a Raw plant-based diet. Our bodies are amazing. In fact, that statement doesn't even do our bodies justice. Our bodies are freakin' phenomenal! Did you know that you are made up of over a hundred trillion cells? A hundred trillion! So, why not feed them the nutrients they need to thrive? When your cells become diseased, they behave in abnormal ways, many of which bring on much pain and suffering. Eating a diet that is high in Raw food can help you fight disease and maintain a healthy immune system. When your immune system is strong, it's generally no problem for you to be in the presence of germs. Germs are opportunistic. This means that they take advantage of you when your guard is down. It is only when your body is not strong enough to fight the germs that you get sick.

Germs seek and thrive in their natural habitat, which is unhealthy, toxic tissue in which there are no natural defenses to kill them. It's this very reason that I don't get stressed when I am around people with a cold or the flu. I don't get anxiety in the winter months when everyone around me is suffering with aches, pains, runny noses and coughs. I'm not threatened by flying in an airplane with the fear that I will "catch something" because my immune system is clean, vibrant and healthy. Most people's pain and misery results from their own poor dietary choices.

According to Henry Bieler, MD, author of "Food Is Your Best Medicine," one of the first questions a woman asks after giving birth is, "Doctor, is my baby alright?" He was so often puzzled by this because he believed that if every mother's desire is to have a truly healthy baby, why do most women typically take such poor care of themselves before even getting pregnant and in many cases, during the pregnant months?

AMERICA'S HEALTH CHALLENGES

Heart Disease

As of 2007, heart disease is the leading cause of death in the United States. I'll bet that is no surprise—you can probably can start rattling off names of people you know who've suffered from conditions related to heart disease.

The frustrating thing, *yet the most glorious thing* about heart disease, is that it's completely preventable—and even reversible! It's frustrating because people (you and I) can actually do something about it and *so many people don't*. It's glorious because it can be stopped in its tracks, which is overwhelmingly empowering, and people are doing this every day through diet. It's amazing how quickly people can recover from heart disease by diet alone.

Studies show that a single bad meal can cause injury to your arteries. Dr. Caldwell Esselstyn of the Cleveland Clinic, one of the world's leading authorities on reversing heart disease through diet, urges that, when it comes to cholesterol, *"moderation kills."* When asked about the effects of an occasional steak or slice of pizza, Dr. Esselstyn says, *"We now know that a single fatty meal compromises coronary flow. This is true even in young people. You can see it with a scan five minutes later."*

Our livers produce all the cholesterol we need, and one of the great things about plants is that they contain zero cholesterol. So many people think they are doing their bodies a favor by eating chicken instead of red meat (to reduce cholesterol), but it isn't so. Chicken has approximately the same amount of cholesterol as red meat. It is simple. Avoid meat.

The risk of developing heart disease among meat-eaters is 50 percent higher than that of vegetarians. According to William Castelli, M.D., director, Framingham Heart Study, the longest-running clinical study in medical history, vegans "have the lowest rates of coronary disease of any group in the country... they have a fraction of our heart attack rate, and they have only 40 percent of our cancer rate." He also states, "We've never had a heart attack in Framingham in 35 years in anyone who had a cholesterol under 150."

One of the things troubling my mind is that many medical authorities are still recommending a diet that is 30% fat, but there is not one instance showing that such a diet has either stopped or reversed heart disease. In fact, that level of fat promotes heart disease. Doctor Castelli states, "A low-fat, plant-based diet would not only lower the heart attack rates by about 85 percent, but it would lower the cancer rate 60 percent." It is no secret that both heart disease and cancer are two hallmarks of animal based diets.

And... one last note... let's talk about sex, baby!

If the standard American diet (high in saturated fat and cholesterol) can block arteries to the heart, brain and all other parts of the body, it should not be surprising that the same diet can block arteries to the entire genital region. Yes, erectile dysfunction ("ED") is commonly caused by lack of blood flow and blocked arteries, typically the result of consuming animal (meat) and animal by-products (eggs and dairy products).

According to a study by the US National Institute on Aging, cholesterol levels are a bigger factor than age in the onset of impotence. And according to the Joslin Diabetes Center at Harvard University, "Diabetes can cause nerve and artery damage in the genital area, disrupting the blood flow necessary for an erection."

Don't let meat destroy your health or ruin your love life. It's not worth it!

Diabetes

Diabetes is a condition where the body cannot efficiently metabolize certain foods, most notably starches and sugars, as a result of a dirty circulatory system. More specifically, when you have too much fat in the blood, it is difficult for glucose to get into your cells and utilized for energy. This plays a huge role in obesity and weight gain as well.

A March, 2003, study published in the journal *Diabetes Care* estimated the costs of diabetes in 2002 at $132 billion with direct medical costs totaling $92 billion. That's a lot of money. And, of all the drug dosage errors made in hospitals in this country, the greatest number of errors is made with insulin because it's tricky trying to figure out the right amount to administer.

The good news is the potential we have (yep, that's you and me) for preventing diabetes is astounding. A whopping 90-95% of all cases of type 2 diabetes are preventable and *even reversible!* Check out *Rawfor30days.com* to see a mind-blowing documentary being made about a group of diabetic patients helping to heal their diabetic conditions with a Raw plant-based diet. It is exhilarating and inspiring.

Cancer

Cancer is scary. I have seen close family and friends suffer with this terrible disease, much of it needlessly. In the United States, breast cancer is now at its highest ever. More and more evidence shows that eating animal protein increases your risk of getting this terrible disease. According to Karen Emmons, M.D., Dana-Farber Cancer Institute, Boston, "Five to ten percent of all cancers are caused by inherited genetic mutations. By contrast, 70 to 80% have been linked to [diet and other] behavioral factors."

What we know is this: Cancer thrives in an acidic environment where there is a lack of oxygen. When you eat food that is acidic by nature, such as animal protein, you make your blood stream more acidic. Hence, limit foods that raise your acidity level, increase alkaline foods (fresh Raw plant-foods) and help prevent cancer, or fight it if you already have it.

Obesity

A friend of mine, a well-known radiologist in Arizona, gave the following speech at a continuing medical education seminar where the focus was wellness, diet and lifestyle.

> *"A topic on everyone's mind today is how to achieve health, or in some cases, how to maintain it. On a daily basis, newspapers and magazines are filled with articles on health, diet and nutrition. Vitamins, diet supplements and potions of all sorts are espoused as elixirs for a long, healthy life. With this*

tidal wave of information, it's often difficult to separate truth from fiction.

"Compounding all of this information and misinformation is the problem of obesity in this country. Sixty-five percent of the U.S. adult population (20 years and older) is either overweight or obese. More frightening, 16% of children and teens in this country, according to the American Heart Association, are overweight. It is a problem that is not going away. In fact, it is accelerating. In 1993, not a single state in the union reported an obesity prevalence rate above 20%. Ten years later in 2003, 31 states had obesity prevalence rates between 20 and 24% and another four states had rates at or above 25%.

"Clearly, we are in the middle of an obesity epidemic and this will result in more cardiovascular disease (already the number one killer), diabetes, hypertension, cancer, degenerative joint disease, etc. Some suggest that if we continue along this same path, the current generation of children could be the first in American history to live shorter lives than their parents."

There are financial consequences to obesity—costs that we all share as individuals, employers and through government-sponsored health programs such as Medicaid and Medicare. Medical expenditures that result from treating obesity-related diseases are significant. According to R. Sturm et al, obese adults between the ages of 20 and 65, have annual medical expenses that are 36% higher than those of normal-weight people. As BMI (body mass index) increases so do the number of sick days, medical claims and healthcare costs. According to Thompson et al, the health-related economic cost to U.S. business is significant, representing about 5% of total medical care costs."

Want some more alarming information? A team at Johns Hopkins University in Baltimore examined 20 studies, and Dr. Youfa Wang, who led the study, said in a statement, "Obesity is a public health crisis. If the rate of obesity and overweight continues at this pace, by 2015, 75 percent of adults and nearly 24 percent of U.S. children and adolescents will be overweight or obese."

Allergies, Osteoporosis and Dairy

I can't write a book about health and not include information about dairy. Dairy is linked with arthritis, heartburn, headaches, osteoporosis, obesity, heart disease, cancer, diabetes, acne and more. It's filled with hormones, steroids, antibiotics and pesticides. It can even contain white blood cells from the cow... in other words, pus. *And people drink it!* That's quite the cocktail to which I say, "no thanks!"

Humans are designed to digest Mother's breast milk... *as babies.* We're the only species drinking milk as adults. Hmmmm... think about it. Do you ever see anywhere in nature an animal that is past its youngest phase in life and still attached to its mother's nipple? No. So, why in the world do we continue to consume dairy when it's made for babies?

Dairy products are full of saturated fats and cholesterol. Often a body will develop a cold or "allergies" to fight the dairy invasion, which is why dairy forms mucus. All you have to do is give up all dairy for just one week. That's it, just one week. Then, go eat a slice of pizza and have some ice cream and see what happens to you the next morning. You'll be filled with phlegm, snot and mucus. Yuck. One of the reasons people get such bad breath in the morning is from the mucus coating their nasal passages and throat. The mucus is a result of undigested lactose and the acidic nature of pasteurized milk. Both of these encourage the growth of bacteria. According to the periodical, *Pediatrics*, "Dairy products may play a major role in the development of allergies, asthma, sleep difficulties, and migraine headaches." I personally know many people who experienced immediate improvement with their allergies and asthma once they stopped consuming dairy. If you suffer from these ailments, try eliminating dairy and see how clearly you can breathe, starting within *just a couple of days!*

Arthritis is another problem for many Americans, and as more and more Baby Boomers start hitting their older years, you're going to hear about this over and over again. Dairy can aggravate arthritis terribly. In controlled studies, dairy products are the most frequently cited food triggers of arthritis! (Has the Dairy Council—which spends millions of dollars on advertising to brainwash us that we need their product—ever made any TV ads telling you that their product actually triggers allergies and arthritis*?!*)

My mom used to suffer from arthritis pain on a daily basis until she eliminated dairy from her diet. There was a time when she couldn't get up from sitting or lying down without experiencing pain from her arthritis. Once she stopped consuming dairy, it was a matter of days and she started to feel immediate improvement.

For people who are concerned about getting enough calcium to prevent osteoporosis and using milk as a means to that end, read this: There is not one study that has found dairy consumption to be a deterrent to osteoporosis.

On the contrary, many doctors and experts in the field have clearly shown that the high protein content of dairy actually leaches calcium from the body. The National Dairy Council *itself* revealed that the high protein content of dairy steals calcium from your bones.

This is because protein is acidic to your body, and in order to help alkalize your system, calcium is taken from the bones and put into the blood. It is no surprise that the countries showing the highest consumption of dairy and meat also have the highest incidence of osteoporosis and hip fractures.

Higher Dairy Consumption Is Highly Correlated with MORE Osteoporosis

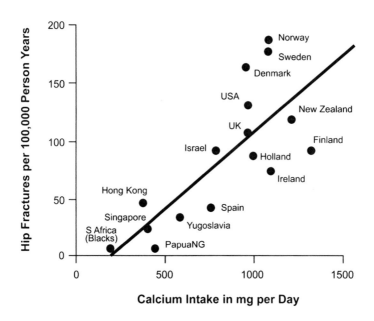

"Populations that consume the most cow's milk and other dairy products have among the highest rates of osteoporosis and hip fracture."

Source: Abelow, Holford and Insogna (1992)

Eskimos, who eat a lot of protein, have some of the highest rates of osteoporosis in the world. According to Neal Barnard, the President of the Physicians Committee for Responsible Medicine, *"Animal protein is one of the biggest predictors of kidney failure and osteoporosis"* and that includes dairy.

If you're looking for ways to get calcium in your diet, then eat fresh Raw foods such as kale, collard greens, mustard greens, cabbage, kelp, seaweed, watercress, broccoli, fruits, nuts and seeds. You also get much higher levels of manganese, chromium, magnesium and selenium from fresh fruits and vegetables. It is that simple. If you need a substitute for dairy when eating your cereal or Raw granola, then try fresh Raw nut or seed milk. This is the most delicious and healthy substitute for unhealthy cow's milk any day.

One of the best books on the subject is *"Milk: A-Z"* by Robert Cohen and one of the best Web sites about the subject is www.milksucks.com.

Stress

Stress creates an acidic condition in the body, which can be a breeding ground for disease. There will always be stress in our lives to some degree, but we can help minimize the effect it has on us physically by eating a diet that is high in Raw foods. Specifically, the nutrients that help us combat stress are vitamin C, B-complex vitamins, calcium, magnesium and digestive enzymes. Eating a varied and well-balanced Raw plant-based diet helps ensure you get plenty of these vitamins and minerals.

Depression

Depression is a horrible mental state that afflicts numerous Americans today. As a result, prescriptions for treating this disease are at an all time high. I am a firm believer that the chemicals found in a lot of processed foods today do wacky things to our brain chemistry and children's brains and can easily contribute to depression. That is why so many people immediately notice an improvement in their mood once they start eliminating junk from their diets and they start eating fresh, vibrant living plant foods. It's no secret that people report a marked increase in happiness, mental clarity and focus when they go Raw.

But there is a less well-known, and perhaps more important, aspect to going Raw. It's an effect that is harder to grasp and fully comprehend until it happens to you personally. If you are new to Raw food, the following may sound strange and a little "out there," but a lot of people — ordinary people like you and me — describe a new and hard-to-define sense of "connection" with their food, once they go Raw. And by extension, they feel a new and different connection to their world, nature, and the role we have on this planet. Imagine feeling *truly* connected! To *everything!* The effects of this take on many forms. It's not at all uncommon, for instance, for people to want to start growing some of their own food. Even people living in downtown high-rise apartments! To many, going Raw is like awakening something deep within, that has always been there, but suppressed.

Now, maybe this quasi-spiritual, transformational experience is the product of simply thinking a lot about diet, in new ways and new contexts. Or maybe it's a by-product of having a healthier, cleaner, toxin-free internal state, which makes you simply feel "good." Or getting great sleep, maybe for the first time in years. But regardless, in many ways, the food we eat is, by far (even more so than the air we breathe), the most direct connection we have to the outside world. The molecules we ingest actually become "us." The old adage is true: "We are what we eat." Literally.

26

Anti-Aging: Mentally & Physically

You'll see that most people who have been living the Raw lifestyle look younger. They have a beautiful glow about them, soft skin, and typically far fewer wrinkles. I attribute this to all of the nutrition they're getting from eating anti-oxidant rich foods, as well as eliminating foods that are acidic and hard on your body (animal flesh, animal by-products, saturated fats, cholesterol, processed foods, high sugar and high fat foods). Start living the Raw lifestyle and you just might find yourself spending a lot less on fancy anti-wrinkle creams, which are full of potentially hazardous chemicals anyway. It's like getting a face-lift from living the Raw lifestyle... gotta love that!

Where aging is concerned, another horrible challenge in our world today has to do with people suffering from Alzheimer's disease. The Raw lifestyle can help here, too. A study in the *American Journal of Medicine* showed that people in their study who drank an 8-ounce glass of fruit or vegetable juice three or more times a week were 76 percent less likely to develop Alzheimer's than those who drank less than one serving. It's those powerful antioxidants and phytonutrients going to work for you all the time.

Sleep Problems

I go back and forth between eating a High Raw and all Raw diet. As a result of eating so much Raw, I have the best and most peaceful sleep ever. For so long I used to think it was normal to wake up in the middle of the night drenched in sweat, even though I went to bed feeling chilly. I would toss and turn throughout the night, blaming my mattress for the unruly sleep. I believed that it was impossible to wake up feeling refreshed. Furthermore, I never imagined a life without my alarm clock. Little did I know that it is during sleep that your body starts to detox and process a lot of what you did during the day. It's during this time that your body begins to repair and build. If you give your body too many toxins to deal with, then your body heats up in the process, making for what is commonly called "digestive fire" while sleeping. This prevents you from getting a good night's sleep. I had my fair share of that during my life (but not anymore).

You may not wake up in a full sweat in the middle of the night, but if you're like most people, you need an alarm clock to wake up. Furthermore, I'll bet that most people don't wake up really refreshed (with or without an alarm clock), ready to bounce out of bed and start the day... at least, not until they get their coffee! Pure restful sleep helps you do this, and in order for your body to get the best sleep, you can't fill it with toxic sludge.

CHAPTER 3

HOW RAW WORKS

After reading the following information about enzymes, nutrients, and the detrimental effect heat has on your food, you will realize that it is a no-brainer as to how and why Raw food is the healthiest cuisine in the world. It just makes sense.

Raw food is the healthiest choice for food because of two main components:

- Phytonutrients

- Digestion with Fiber, Water and Enzymes

Phytonutrients and enzymes are both destroyed with high levels of heat—enzymes start to "denature" (get mangled) around 115 degrees and phytonutrients start to become less bio-available at 130 degrees. Therefore, to ensure you're eating the healthiest food, it's important to not use heat that is higher than 115 degrees.

PHYTONUTRIENTS

The most fundamental component of the Raw food lifestyle and why it is the healthiest cuisine in the world has to do with vitamins and phytonutrients. Phytonutrients, which means "plant nutrients" (also known as "phyto-chemicals,") are biologically active compounds that help you fight and prevent disease. Thankfully, these smart little helpers are starting to get much more recognition these days among scientists and, to some extent, the media (and one day, maybe policy-makers... oh well). They are known to fight directly against viruses and bacteria, as well as promoting a healthy immune system, and helping to fight the process of aging. No wonder all those Raw vegans look so young!

One of the most important functions of phytonutrients is in the form of antioxidants, which are necessary to help fight any free radicals in your body (free radicals cause damage to you and accelerate your aging). A study from UCLA/Louisiana State University of more than 17,500 men and women showed the consumption of salad and raw vegetables correlates with higher levels of folic acid, vitamins C and E, lycopene, and alpha and beta carotene in the bloodstream. Another study, from the American Journal of Clinical Nutrition, shows that apples and pears rank very high for fighting heart disease. They have high levels of flavonoids, which are anti-inflammatory and support a healthy heart.

The trick to phytonutrients however is that most are heat sensitive and they start to become less bio-available with heat, more specifically, temperatures of about 130 degrees. So, if you eat cooked veggies and think you are getting lots of phytonutrients and vitamins, then think again... because you're not. They've been destroyed and cannot be brought back to life. You are eating empty calories. Organic mush.

One of the ways fresh organic Raw food helps you get to and maintain your perfect weight is that it is full of nutrition, of which most people are typically starved. When eating a diet that is primarily cooked (and destroys nutrients), people often find themselves hungry, because their bodies need not more calories, but rather, *the nutrition.* I see people spending money every month for supplements and vitamins, when they could have been getting it all along with fresh organic produce (and probably saving a bunch of money at the same time!).

Last but not least, phytonutrients are responsible for giving fruits and vegetables their gorgeous vibrant colors. This makes them so pleasing to the eye, and this is important for your mindset. In real estate, they say it's all about "location, location, location"... well, when it comes to food, it's all about "presentation, presentation, presentation." Your new Raw plant-based breakfasts, lunches and dinners, with all of their beautiful radiant colors, will be sure to please your eyes, as well as your tastes.

DIGESTION & ENZYMES

It's often said, "look at a person's digestive system and you'll see his level of health." When you eat cooked or processed foods devoid of their natural enzymes, as well as water, it's harder on your body to digest the food. Enzymes are the power of life. They are living forces that conduct and direct every activity in your body. Enzymes are made of amino acids and are critical for life. Basically, without enzymes, you cease to exist. Digestive enzymes help "digest" or break down foods. The funny thing is this has been known for a long time. It just was not given as much recognition as it is today. Many people believe eating an enzyme-rich diet is also thought to increase vitality and slow the aging process.

While more research is needed to fully understand the processes involved, one of the most common hypotheses given for why people experience high energy with Raw food is that the body does not spend as much time digesting it. Digestion is the body's number one energy drainer. If you can facilitate that process you will feel more pure, real energy. I'm sure you have experienced getting sleepy after eating cooked food. This is because your digestive system is overworked by trying to process it. It's not uncommon for cooked food to take anywhere from 1-4 days to go through the entire digestive system and get eliminated. Or as I like to say... it takes 1-4 days to go from the "roota-to-the-toota." All this time, your body is working hard to process and assimilate the food, drawing upon energy and enzymes to do that. Conversely, when you eat fresh, Raw food, it takes as little as 20 minutes and up to maybe 6 hours to be digested (depending on food combining... for instance, melons, when eaten alone, move very quickly through your system).

The bottom line: When you cook food, you're destroying nutrients and enzymes. It is like eating empty foods that just fill you up temporarily, providing you with fuel but little else of what the body needs to maintain cellular health. You cause your body to do more work than necessary to digest the cooked food.

PROTEIN

For too long, we have been misguided and programmed to believe that the only source of protein is from meat — aka, animal tissue. In reality, plant-based foods contain plenty of high-quality protein that is easier for your body to digest and assimilate. The reason they are higher quality is simple: Plant proteins are found inside plant cells, the walls of which are made of the rigid material we call fiber. Fiber passes through our system in a nice, orderly fashion, giving us healthy, regular bowel movements. In contrast, animal proteins are inside of animal cells, the walls of which are made of cholesterol, and our bodies aren't well-equipped to break it down. It coats our gut with grease, making absorption difficult. It constipates us. And when absorbed into our blood, cholesterol makes our blood thick, clogs our arteries, and kills more Americans than anything else. By eating a variety of plants in your diet, including plenty of greens, it is very easy to get 100% "complete" protein, meaning all 8 essential amino acids are present in abundance. It's all about quality versus quantity when it comes to protein, because a high protein diet can be dangerous.

32

Think of this: Humans have one of the lowest requirements for protein. Even as a baby, when you are most in need of protein for growth... even then, the food designed for you, mother's breast milk, only has about two percent protein. That is all babies need, and they have the highest need for protein of all humans, because they grow faster than people of any other age. Coincidentally—or perhaps not so coincidentally—this is typically the same percentage found in... *guess what?*... most fruits and vegetables.

Cooked protein is extremely harmful because the protein becomes damaged (causing it to congeal and denature), meaning the protein molecules change their composition to something that is actually less usable to the body. People who eat cooked protein find themselves needing more protein on a daily basis, because their bodies can only assimilate a portion of the cooked protein. Unfortunately, they turn to sources *of more* cooked protein, or supplements, to make up for it, furthering their spiral downward into unhealthy territory. Your body can assimilate protein more easily from Raw food than cooked food. Therefore, the consensus of many leading authorities is that quality is far more important than quantity. When you eat fresh, Raw plant-based protein sources, your body is able to assimilate the amino acids more efficiently because they're not destroyed or denatured by heat. Therefore, *you do not need as much.* Raw protein is considered more digestible by the human body. The amino acids and digestive enzymes are intact; whereas cooked foods are devoid of these enzymes. They are denatured, making them more likely to sit in the colon, essentially rotting, increasing the risk for disease. (This is why carnivores, such as lions, have much shorter digestive tracts than vegan animals such as humans—to allow meat to be processed and excremented as quickly as possible.) Excess protein can harm your digestive tract, steal calcium from your bones, drain you of energy, and cause you to easily gain weight. Moreover, high protein and fat consumption are linked to cancer, heart disease, arthritis, kidney and liver problems, osteoporosis, diabetes and obesity.

People often ask me about eating raw meat. While it's true that the enzymes are intact in raw meat, it introduces a host of other issues, most notably, parasite susceptibility and other poisons. Fish is especially dangerous. Heavy metals that pollute our oceans are absorbed by the fish, making it toxic. The flesh of fish can accumulate toxins up to 9 *million times* as concentrated as those in the waters they live in! Additionally, fish on farms are often fed antibiotics. According to the Centers for Disease Control and Prevention, 325,000 people get sick and some die every year in the U.S. from eating contaminated fish and other sea animals. This information should be reason enough to stop eating animal-based foods.

How much protein does a person need? The World Health Organization (WHO) recommends that only about 10% of our calories come from protein. People act so concerned about getting enough protein, that you'd think that "protein deficiency" was... um, an actual problem in our culture. Huh? Where is this problem exactly? Show me somebody who doesn't get enough protein, but otherwise eats enough food. Put it this way—in your whole life—have you ever met anybody (who isn't starving in general) that is protein deficient?

Protein deficiency is simply *not* part of our culture's reality. The world's longest living cultures, Okinawans and the Hunzas of Pakistan for example—who frequently live to be over 100 years old—consume only small amounts of protein.

The bottom line: Try it and see how well it works for you. You will be amazed at how much more energy you have when you eat a diet high in Raw organic foods such as fresh fruits, vegetables, nuts and seeds. You won't feel dragged down as a result of your body trying to digest cooked and denatured protein. Even bottomless-pit growing teenagers and competitive athletes are able to get totally adequate amounts of protein on a Raw vegan diet.

CARBOHYDRATES

Carbohydrates are something to be loved, not feared. Glucose is the natural fuel for our bodies. Natural sugar foods, such as fresh raw fruit, fuel our brain, cognition, and most other functions. Before our cells can use *any* food as fuel, it needs to be converted into simple sugars. Carbohydrates happen to be the easiest to convert into simple sugars, as opposed to fats and proteins.

Carbohydrates are therefore extremely important to your body. The best and most nutritious carbohydrates you can get are in the form of fruit (both sweet and non-sweet) as well as vegetables. (It's important to know that any plant with seeds is considered a fruit. Therefore, cucumbers, tomatoes, zucchini, etc are all considered non-sweet varieties of fruit.)

Our cultural fear of carbohydrates exists because we have come to associate the word "carbohydrates" with what you may have heard called "Empty Carbs"—that is, nutritionally bankrupt carbohydrate sources comprising primarily grains and starchy foods such as wheat flour, corn, bread, pasta, cookies, cake, mashed potatoes, doughnuts, and so on. All of these have several things in common that makes them appropriately feared and a veritable recipe for getting fat. These foods are:

- Low in nutrition

- Low in fiber

- Low in water

- Very high in calories

- Yummy to babies, who then become addicted for life, even prompting us to invent the term *"comfort food"*

In other words, when you eat these Empty Carbs, you are filling up not on good, necessary things like water and fiber, but on one thing: sugar. Almost pure suger. No wonder then, that if you eat any of these foods until you "feel full," you will have just gotten far more calories than you need to maintain your weight, but still be deficient in essential nutrients, which leads you to quickly feel hungry again, just as soon as your stomach is no longer bursting at the seams. Other than gulping down a few sticks of butter, eating these foods is perhaps the fastest ways to create a caloric surplus, which is to say, gain fatty weight. (Your body converts and stores unused carbohydrates into the fat that deposits around your waste, butt—and heart.)

The important point is this: The carbohydrates found in fruits and vegetables are not to be feared. That is because they come pre-packaged in *good proportions* with other things that fill you up, signaling you to stop eating—specifically, fiber, water, and nutrients. Fiber and water take up a lot of room and physically make your stomach feel full. Stomach fullness is one of several of the body's satiety cues (along with blood sugar levels and jaw fatigue from chewing), meaning your brain wants to stop eating. Nutrients operate on longer timeframes such as hours or days: If you have enough of a given nutrient, your body stops craving foods high in those nutrients.

If controlling your weight is ever a problem, remember this one thing, and it will change your life: The trick to being able to eat a comfortable amount—essentially "as much as you feel like eating"—is to eat foods that *fill you up* with stuff other than pure sugar (or fat). In other words, fiber and water. In other words again, fruits and vegetables. It boils down to the simple math of calories per unit of volume, and your stomach has a finite amount of space.

In practice, if you're trying to lose weight and you have a craving for something hearty and comforting like spaghetti—before giving in, first eat your fill of salad or drink a green smoothie. Once your stomach is full, the bad food won't seem nearly as appetizing.

FATS

Raw plant fats are very helpful in transitioning you to living the Raw lifestyle, away from cooked foods. The healthiest plant fats come in the whole food form, such as fresh avocados, nuts, seeds, and olives. "Good fats" can bind with toxins, helping to eliminate them from your body, making these some of the most healing fats for the body. If you are looking for essential fatty acids, then look no further than hemp foods, flax seeds, and walnuts.

Within reason, you will not get fat by eating avocados, sprouted nuts and seeds, and other plant fats. Everything in moderation of course—don't eat ten avocados at every meal and expect to lose weight—but eating sensible portions of these foods frequently is not an issue for most people with respect to weight.

Because moderate amounts of fat in its raw state is assimilated and digested properly, it is not likely to clog the blood and arteries or cause chronic and degenerative diseases like cooked fats can do.

When I use a Raw oil in my recipes, I prefer Raw organic olive oil, hemp oil, flax oil and coconut oil. Make sure to get centrifuged olive oil and virgin or centrifuged coconut oil. To see my favorite brands, visit KristensRaw.com/store.

The bad fats people usually encounter include trans-fats, saturated animal fat, and refined polyunsaturated fats, such as refined cooking oils. The good, natural fats (hemp and flax, for example) are very sensitive to heat and are easily damaged by it. Heated fats lose their antioxidant qualities and are classified as carcinogenic. Furthermore, when people think they are getting omegas from cooked salmon, they should reconsider; omegas are among the most heat-sensitive of all fats.

GREENS

Let's look at greens, because they're powerful. And I mean *super powerful.*

When referring to greens as nutritious, it's predominantly because of their abundance of chlorophyll. This is the green pigment molecule in plants and is responsible for absorbing the sun's energy for photosynthesis. The chlorophyll molecule in plants is chemically similar to hemoglobin in human blood. The only difference in the two molecules is that the central atom in chlorophyll is magnesium, whereas in humans it is iron. (Isn't that cool? We animals are more closely related to plants than you'd have thought.) As a food supplement, chlorophyll can detoxify and purify the blood and liver, help build red blood cells and aid in tissue repair.

Probably the most powerful green available is wheat grass. This is a type of grass that can be juiced and drunk straight (this is intense!) or added to juice and smoothies. Wheat grass that is certified organic produces very high concentrations of chlorophyll, enzymes and vitamins. (Be aware that non-organic wheat grass is very likely to be a nutritionally diminished version of the real thing.) It is a plant that has the nutrient profile similar to that of other leafy green vegetables and contains vitamins A, B complex, C, and E; trace elements calcium, iron, magnesium, and potassium; enzymes; and amino acids. As an antioxidant, organic wheat grass can boost the immune system and soak up free radicals. Organic wheat grass has been shown to be a powerful body detoxifier. Its high chlorophyll content cleanses the liver, tissues and cells, and purifies the blood. Organic wheat grass also contains folic acid, iron, and vitamin B-12, which are required for proper red blood cell production.

I've been asked before whether it is possible to eat too many greens. In my opinion, balance is the key to everything. It is important to rotate the foods you eat, including greens. A great way to do this easily is by eating seasonally with your produce. Another way, for greens especially, is to vary the greens you eat each week. You'll find that chomping and chomping on endless amounts of greens results in masseter fatigue (a tired jaw muscle). Again, this is one of the body's satiety cues, meaning you'll naturally be inclined to stop eating. If you want more greens in your diet, but you are tired of chewing them, then two other options are 1) juice the greens, which extracts the fiber (plant pulp), allowing you to consume more greens, and therefore, more nutrients and 2) make green smoothies where you blend (in a blender) the greens, typically with some fruit to make it taste better.

CHAPTER 4

ORGANICS

"Organic" refers to the way agricultural products are grown and processed. The goal in organic farming is to maintain and replenish the soil fertility without using toxic pesticides, herbicides, or fertilizers. "Certified Organic" means the item has been grown in accordance with strict uniform standards that are verified by an independent state or private organization.

Dr. Alan Greene of Stanford's Children's Hospital neatly summarizes the argument for organics:

> *"Eat organic produce. Your immune system won't waste energy trying to fight off the toxins that are sprayed on conventional fruits and vegetables."*

Eating organics frees up your immune system and antioxidants to do their evolutionarily evolved job, which is to fight off pathogens, cancer, and other diseases originating from natural environmental sources. Your body's natural defense mechanisms are incredibly strong, but like anything else, they can only handle so much attack. To keep your defensive line from being spread too thin, you should therefore limit exposure to toxins (and stress) as much as possible. It's important to realize that consuming pesticides and herbicides—even if they have not been found to be directly carcinogenic—can, in effect, lead to cancer if they use up your supply of antioxidants, which would otherwise have prevented cancer that was generated from another source.

It's true that organic foods typically cost more than conventional, but this may be true only in the short-term. After you adopt a healthier lifestyle with healthier food choices, including organics, you may find yourself frequenting the doctor's office much less (like, never) and spending less on medications (like, none)— over the counter and prescriptions— and not to mention a lower chance of finding yourself prematurely dead.

It's important to know that organically produced foods must meet rigorous governing regulations in all aspects of production. Organic food production is labor and management-intensive, usually produced on smaller farms, which don't benefit from economies of scale. These factors combined, cause the cost to be higher. But as the saying goes, "you get what you pay for." And not to wax overly political, but these amazing foods require more manual labor, such as removing pests by hand in some cases, and organic farmers are hit much harder than big factory farms by policies that restrict access to adequate amounts of immigrant labor. Just something to keep in mind when you look at the price of food that hasn't been dowsed in carcinogenic chemicals.

I can usually only buy organic for the food I prepare myself (and this included my oils, spices, and herbs). Unfortunately, most restaurants don't use organic food... very disappointing, but hopefully this will change over time. If enough customers (read: you, your friends, your family, strangers you preach to on the streets, etc.) demanded organic every time they ordered food, more producers would produce it, and prices would come down. So, start voting with your dollar. When you go to a restaurant and you're paying the bill, take a moment to fill out the comment card, or write directly on the receipt, that you would eat there more often if they offered some organic foods. Or my favorite (and likely much more effective), when your server takes your drink order, ask if they have any organic wines. If they do, order some. If they don't, say, "Okay, I'll just have water." If this happened just three times a week, per waiter, per restaurant, then organic wines would be ubiquitous in restaurants in just a few months. Remember, you're the customer. Restaurant management can't read your mind. You must let them know what you want. This is how we make a difference.

CHAPTER 5

EXPECTATIONS

A great many things await you when you go Raw. People quickly experience weight loss, increased energy, soft skin, clear and bright eyes, silky hair, better sleep, mental clarity, major health improvements, a peaceful mindset and much more.

As with many things in life, whether it's diet, religion, etc., there are many different camps of thought as to which is the best plan. This can be very confusing for people, as it was for me. There are people on the extreme end of the Raw spectrum that are classified as "Natural Hygienists" and they lead a fairly strict lifestyle. Many of them don't use salt, garlic or even ginger in their food. So, you can imagine that their position on something like agave nectar will not be favorable. This is fine for them. But, it might not be fine for you. On the other end of the Raw spectrum is where you find people eating anywhere from 75% to 99% of their diet as Raw and they classify themselves as "High Raw." Of course, there are people who call themselves 100% Raw and they eat anything (plant-based) that is Raw (agave nectar, raw cacao, raw nuts and seeds, etc). I think labels can be difficult unless you know hard and fast how you will eat and that you'll stay that way. I find that many people evolve until they find what works best for themselves and their family. If you eat 100% Raw every day of the month except one or two days, does that suddenly mean you can't classify yourself as Raw? That would be harsh in my opinion. And what if it changes over the years?

It all depends where you are on your journey and what your goals are. If your life recently included eating cooked desserts, then, in my opinion, a Raw dessert such as chocolate mousse made with agave nectar is a far superior choice than what you may have eaten in the past. However, your food style may change as you continue on the road of Raw food. I always say, "listen to your own body" because you'll figure it out and notice what you like, what is easy for you, and what makes you feel the best.

There are a lot of books available with plenty of different opinions about Raw food. My meta-position: I don't take any one position all the way. Everyone is different and might react differently to certain foods. However, there is one common denominator—the more Raw plant-based food people eat, the better they feel. If the ideas I present in this book were yarns, it would be up to you to weave your own blanket.

"One of the most tragic things I know about human nature is that all of us tend to put off living. We are all dreaming of some magical rose garden over the horizon-instead of enjoying the roses blooming outside our windows today."

— Dale Carnegie

DETOXIFICATION

Detoxification is the process whereby the body eliminates stored toxins. Very often, when you stop ingesting new toxins (such as by converting to a cleaner, toxin-free diet), your body seizes the opportunity to clean house of all of the garbage that has been accumulating. In the informal lingo of nutrition, this is known as "detoxing."

It's likely that you'll experience detox in some form when you start eating a diet that is high in fresh Raw food. The best thing you can do is be prepared and know in advance that it's not a permanent phenomenon. Part of being prepared is simply knowing what to expect. One size does not fit all here; it varies for people, based on current dietary habits, individual history, behaviors, environment, and genes. Your experience will differ from another's because of what toxins you might already have in you, plus your current lifestyle.

After a period of time, the body builds up toxins and natural waste products from chemicals, pollution and indulging in foods that are harder for the body to handle. A process of cleansing the internal system, or "detoxifying," helps rid the body of harmful chemicals that may be contributing to fatigue, illness, pain, and poor digestion. When you remove toxin-laden foods from your diet, the body's resources are freed up to remove toxins that have been building up in the body, often for many years. During detoxification, the body eliminates these built-up toxins the same way it always does, through your eliminative organs: the skin, bowel, urinary tract, etc. Shifting to a vegan and/or Raw diet therefore is often initially accompanied by cold or allergy-like symptoms, particularly the production of phlegm. This is temporary and also can be quite a satisfying experience once you realize that the mucus your body is expelling is literally garbage that you have been carrying around in your tissue for a long time. And once it's out, it's out, leaving your cleansed body in a much healthier, cleaner, efficient state.

Here are some examples of what people have experienced when going through detox from a Raw diet:

- Bloating

- Skin eruptions and acne-like symptoms

- Headaches

- Body aches

- Runny nose and cold-like symptoms

- Extreme fatigue

- Mood swings and flaring emotions

- Weight loss

- And more...

One of my favorite experiences when going Raw was the cleansing and detox period. Hard to believe? Yes, this can be painful for some people. It was no picnic for me either. I had my share of headaches, pain, snotty nose, skin rashes and horrible tiny pimples... my face suddenly looked like sandpaper with all the little bumps. I thought, "Where did these come from?" I instinctively knew it was the detox and I felt relief to seeing it expelled and leave my body. Scary, of course, because I realized that I had been carrying those toxins around inside of me for a long time. It was liberating, wonderful, exhilarating (even if I was tired and in pain). It was worth it. I wish I had taken photos of my detox... how about that for a reminder of what not to eat if you are craving something unhealthy? So... detox was arduous, but glorious. Best of all, it typically doesn't last long.

If you're tough and you want to accelerate the detoxification period, then greatly reduce or remove all overt fat from your Raw diet. This means the only fat you'll be consuming is fat found naturally in its whole food form and very little of it. Basically, you'll be eating mostly fruits (sweet and non sweet), vegetables, and keeping your fat level at about ten percent of your total daily calories. To avoid fats during this period, greatly reduce your consumption of nuts, seeds, avocados, and oils (olive, coconut, etc.).

"Fasting" is when you eat no solid foods, and instead drink either water-only, fruit-juice-only, green-juice-only, or some other "only," depending on what type of fast you're doing. Due to its fast and intense impact on the body, fasting, in its various forms, often produces the most dramatic detoxification effects, as the body is finally able to cleanse its digestive tract from years of toxin and mucous build-up quickly and efficiently. During fasting detoxification, the effects are more severe and range from bad breath, to a pasty, white coating of the tongue, to scary-looking things in your bowel movement. Nasty, to be sure, but that is precisely why we want to get this gunk out of our systems. When the detox symptoms disappear, the body is clean, prompting some people to continue the fast until detox symptoms disappear. Common examples are the white tongue returning to pink, or a cessation of scary things in the bowel movement.

WEIGHT LOSS

I've tried almost every diet out there and I never once succeeded with *healthy, long-term, feel-good* weight loss... until I went Raw. Losing weight through anything other than a plant-based plan is the result of bodily distress, meaning it's probably not for the long-term and you will gain it back. And, if it is long-term, your body pays the heavy price for it later, because you've stressed it in such an unhealthy way that you pay the consequences eventually.

Need more proof? Check this out: *The American Cancer Society* conducted a study over a ten-year period with eighty-thousand people trying to lose weight. The participants who ate meat three times a week gained substantially more weight than those who didn't and ate more vegetables. Another study published in the *New England Journal of Medicine* stated that meat eaters are much more likely to be overweight than vegetarians. Eating meat is not the answer to losing weight. (Atkins results are generally temporary, for instance, and according to Brian Wansink, Ph.D., author of "Mindless Eating," similar weight loss can be seen in diets that restrict what you eat to *any* one food—say, corn—because your body naturally gets tired of eating just one food and you stop eating.)

One of the reasons that weight loss is so easy with the Raw food diet has to do with how the food is assimilated and digested in your body. One of the reasons Americans are always hungry is because they are actually not getting the proper nutrition their bodies need. If you find yourself hungry all the time like I used to, it's because your body is crying out for nutrients. Listen to your body! Almost all vitamins and nutrients can only be found in fresh Raw food (B12 being the exception, discussed in Ch.7, *Raw Questions*). And, because Raw food has the nutrients intact, then your body can properly assimilate them. When this happens, your hunger tends to decrease.

I used to be a big food worshipper with an over-the-top appetite. I used to proudly boast to my male friends that I could "out-eat" them... not the most feminine challenge. At the buffets I would bring back 2-3 plates in one trip and I would use a dinner size plate for the dessert table. I used to be so consumed by food, that it was not uncommon for me to think about what I was going to eat for lunch when it was only breakfast, as well as eagerly anticipating dinner before my lunch even started. I used to be *obsessed* with food.

Being in shape and maintaining a healthy, slim waistline was, and still is, important to me. I feel the healthiest, sexiest, and have the most energy when I'm not carrying around extra weight. Therefore, always being excited about food, eating a lot, AND trying to stay slim made that part of my life quite a challenge in the past. That, however, was before going Raw. Since going Raw, my appetite has reduced significantly and I don't obsess about my meals way in advance. There were times in the beginning stages, when I was transitioning from cooked to Raw (and, I'm sure the same will happen to you), when I continued to eat the same quantity of food, even though it was

Raw (which was still a lot). At that point, it was more of a mental game than a physical hunger I was struggling with. When you say good-bye to something in your life, it can be a tough transition for your mind, so take your time doing this and enjoy the journey.

Raw can seem like a huge change, and indeed it is if you go 100% all at once. But, you don't have to go 100% in the beginning (or maybe ever for that matter) to have some amazing results. Just start eating "more" Raw and listen to your body as you go. You're not only putting great food into your body, you'll also stop eating all kinds of garbage (cholesterol, saturated fats, processed sugars, etc.). You'll start feeling better and better and better.

This is a completely new approach to food, lifestyle, and health. It's not really about counting calories anymore, which will be a welcome relief to many people. In fact, it is not complicated at all because all you have to do is eat Raw. As much as you want, within reason. There are no formulas to memorize or carry around with you. No rules about which foods to eat, or at which times of day. It's about feeling your cells work wonders and experiencing your body firing on all cylinders.

ARE YOU STILL HUNGRY?

Some people are very eager to lose weight as quickly as possible. If this is you, here are a couple of tips to help:

- Eat apples. Apples will tend to fill you up quickly and sufficiently because of their pectin. Sometimes I like to eat an apple or two about twenty minutes before a meal. This really helps me eat a lot less. It's very effective to do this before going to a restaurant because it gently raises your blood sugar, which tells your brain that you are full. This way you won't feel deprived when other people are eating some of your former favorite foods because you will be quite satiated.

- Drink fresh organic smoothies as snacks when you are hungry (make them green and filled with minerals or make them with just fruit—whatever you're in the mood for). This does the trick every time! If you can't make a smoothie, then grab a piece of fruit.

- Drink warm miso soup.

- Drink herbal tea (ginger or peppermint are my favorites) with a little agave nectar or stevia, if you like. There's something satiating about this that helps "take the edge off." You won't need this all the time, but it's especially helpful in the beginning, as you transition.

- Brush your teeth. Most people find they're not as excited to eat something after brushing. As a reminder, keep a toothbrush with some all natural toothpaste with you at all times.

ENERGY

Get ready for some explosive energy when you start living the Raw food lifestyle. Having excellent digestion, proper nutrition, and peaceful sleep all contribute to giving you sky-rocketing, pure energy that lasts all day long.

Most Americans consume too much protein, and this is one of the main reasons people always feel so sluggish and tired. Animal protein is an energy drainer because it's hard for your body to digest. Dr. Andrew Weil stated that when his patients come to him with lack of energy, one of the first recommendations he gives is to reduce their consumption of animal protein.

One of the other reasons Americans are always tired is from coming off the highs of caffeine, which causes exhaustion. Personally, I was a victim of both too much protein and adrenal exhaustion from all the caffeine and stimulants I was consuming. My lack of energy was, in fact, one of the driving forces behind my search for healthier living. I was tired of always being tired. It was to the point that I was downing 2-3 triple large soy cappuccinos daily. I knew that was unhealthy and it scared me.

Now, I am at the point where I have tons of energy and it lasts all day. I wake up naturally, without my alarm clock, ready to take on the day. I don't need caffeine to get my brain functioning, because I'm not groggy when I wake up. I am focused and alert. It's a wonderful feeling.

"The difference between one man and another is not mere ability, it is energy."

— Thomas Arnold

DIGESTION

Digestion Timeline

There are 100 million nerves in your intestine. This is not something you want to clog up or coat with toxic sludge. After you eat a meal, blood is shunted to your digestive system, and away from the muscles, brain, and other organs. This is the reason people often feel like resting after eating a big cooked meal as opposed to going out for a jog. When cooked food is in your system too long, it can ferment and putrefy, causing indigestion, heartburn and weight gain. In contrast, fruits and vegetables, which are mostly water, take only a short time traveling through the digestive tract. I feel so great after eating

Raw food and I never feel like I have to "recover," like I did when I ate cooked, hard-to-digest food.

Time needed to get cooked animal food vs. fresh, Raw plant food through your digestive system:

- Steak - 2-3 days (and basically has to rot to get out of your digestive tract)

- Raw Fruit and vegetables: Less than half a day

POOPING... A Direct Link to Your Health

While we're on the topic of digestion and elimination, let's talk about poop. Here is a good rule of thumb: You should be sitting on the porcelain goddess to poop about the same number of times as you eat in a day. Yes, you read that correctly! So, if you're eating 4 meals a day, you should poop about 3-4 times a day, too. It varies a little for each person depending on how you combined your food, how much liquid you are consuming, etc... but this gives you an idea. Now, when I tell people this in my classes, I usually see some jaws drop. All this time they considered themselves lucky to poop once a day! And, here I was telling them they should be doing it 3-4 times a day. This is especially true when starting the Raw diet. You will probably have so much poop and waste backed up in your body that it could take many trips to the toilet before you get with a regular routine.

Things to Help Your Digestion... TODAY

The following are some tips to help your digestion right away so that you can start feeling better immediately.

- Chew your food to a mush. This helps make your food close to liquid, which helps save your body energy when digesting it. I know you have all heard this before, but it is "tested, tried, and true" so start doing it. I used to always forget to do this. The only way I found that would help me remember was to write on a post-it note "CHEW FOOD TO A MUSH" and stick it to any place where I ate (dining room table, desk, night stand, kitchen counter). It worked. It only took about 2 weeks of having those post-it notes around until it became a habit.

- Do not drink liquids within a half hour of eating food or up to an hour after your meal. This might seem counterintuitive. There was a time when people used to drink a big glass of water right before a meal so that it would help "fill them up" and they would eat less (in trying to lose weight). However, we know now that this is harmful to your precious digestive system. When you drink liquids, you dilute your own natural digestive juices, which makes it harder for your body to digest the food.

- Soak your Raw nuts and seeds before eating them. This is important for optimal digestion. It is not required, but definitely recommended. Details about the importance of this and how to do it are provided later in this book.

- Eat melons alone. There are a number of proper food combining principles for food digestion, but I would rank most of them in the "advanced" category (covered later in the book). Eating melons alone, however, is the one that I want you concerned with now. Any time you eat watermelon, cantaloupe, honeydew melon, etc, always try to eat them by themselves. After eating melon, do not eat any other food for at least 25-30 minutes. And, do not eat any melons within four hours after eating anything with high fat or high protein. The ideal time to eat melons is first thing in the morning, after you've spent the night sleeping (naturally fasting).

You will find that this not only aids in digestion, but prevents gas and abdominal discomfort.

MIGRAINES

I suffered from the most horrendous migraine headaches. I was taking very strong prescription pain medications at the early age of 14 to help ease the debilitating pain just so I could go to school. Migraines, and headaches in general, are typically the result of an acidic, toxic body. When people go through detox, they can experience awful headaches. The toxins that have been stored in your tissue are released into the blood stream (and boy do you feel those toxins!) usually in the form of body aches and head pains. If you are currently living a lifestyle that is acidic in nature (stress, diet, pollution, allergies, etc.) then it is no surprise that your body responds in kind with a headache. Usually the first response is to medicate and take the pain away. However, this is merely a band-aid to temporarily help. You have to eventually pay the price for medicating yourself, which also adds to the acidic condition coursing through your body (pain pills are acidic to your body). Of all people, I can appreciate that a headache can cause you to lose time. You can't function completely. You can't focus. However, stay strong. The headache will pass eventually, you just need to give it time. Hopefully, you have a place you can lie down, in the dark, and relax until the pain ceases. Be confident that soon you will probably be rid of all your headaches.

Now that I'm eating a 100% plant-based diet that is mostly Raw, I rarely get headaches. In fact, the only time I might get one is when I go off my High Road of Health.

Here are some things that you might try, to help ease the pain if you have headaches, especially if you are detoxing:

- There is a very effective acupressure technique in which you firmly (until it's slightly uncomfortable) pinch the tendons deep in the 'V' between your thumb and index finger. Do it on both hands or have someone do it for you. This releases endorphins in the brain. You'll often start to feel the headache go away within a minute or two.

- Drink warm herbal tea

- Take a warm bath with the lights low and soft music playing (or no music)

- Get your feet rubbed

- Get a massage

- Rub your temples and/or eyebrows with gentle pressure

- Stretch and breathe deeply

- Sometimes a little food can help, diverting blood from the brain to the stomach

- Drink fresh, alkalizing green juice

WOMEN'S CORNER: RAW AND MENSTRUATION

There has been some excellent research on the effect of diet and a woman's menstrual cycle. Most notably is how the menstruation period (and the common pains associated with it) is greatly reduced when following a low-fat, Raw plant-based diet. Dr. George Starr, M.D., states, "Nothing influences a woman's monthly flow more than diet."

The most unhealthy women experience the hardest, most painful and longest periods of menstruation. It is thought that menstruation is a result of a toxic condition of the blood, which is evident by the leukocyte counts found in the menstrual discharge. Leukocyte count increases when there is poisoning or toxins in the body. Additionally, there is a high loss of sex hormones during the menstruation period, which Dr. Frank, gynecologist in New York, believes this is a main cause for menopause to begin much sooner than necessary. Furthermore, according to Dr. Bieler, "The normal menopause in the healthy woman is almost symptomless." Wow.

Since adopting this healthy lifestyle, my menstrual cycle occurs like clockwork and with much more manageable periods, shorter in duration with less severe pain and PMS. I sure wish I had learned about this ten years ago!

CHAPTER 6

EXERCISE & PHYSICAL FITNESS

"A strong body makes the mind strong."

— Thomas Jefferson

Exercise and physical activity should be an important part of your life—a priority— just like sleeping, eating, drinking water, and resting. It should be a part of your every week, if not every day. If you're frowning at this thought, don't. Exercise and physical fitness is fun and addictive. If you're not already doing it, there will be a point, soon in fact, when you will crave exercise and physical fitness. Physical activity is not limited to just going to the gym. Exercise can be filled with fun activities like playing with your kids at the park, shopping (lots of walking and carrying your bags of purchased goods), walking your dog, dancing, hula-hooping, swimming, jumping rope, and so much more.

In this section, I will give some great tips and tricks to help you get started. However, if you are looking for a more thorough book on exercise and weight loss with Raw fitness, then check out my book, *Kristen Suzanne's Raw Vegan Diet for EASY Weight Loss*.

You will get much more out of Raw when you add physical fitness to your lifestyle. It is about strengthening your body from the inside out. You'll find yourself with so much energy that you will *want* to exercise. You'll want to get outside and enjoy yourself. As you transition to a higher Raw diet, you will find yourself *wanting* to move around. You'll feel so good, you won't be content to just sit on the couch and watch TV. It becomes a virtuous cycle—eating the Raw food makes you want to work out; working out makes you want to eat more Raw! This is how people get sucked into a full swing Raw lifecycle and start making dramatic changes in a way that feels totally transformational, yet in many ways feels effortless because your body naturally tells you what to do next.

One of the main benefits of exercise is that it helps oxygen flow through your body and accelerates your lymph system, which is the body's way of getting rid of cellular waste products and toxic garbage. You end up sweating and removing wastes through your skin. Some experts actually blame cellulite on toxic lymph accumulation. So, eat healthy and pure, fresh organic foods, and get physically active to keep your lymph system flowing.

I have a lot of experience with fitness, strength training, and losing weight. As a former National Physique Committee member, and winner of many bodybuilding trophies, I have learned a lot over the years. According to studies, one session of exercise lowers blood pressure for 24 hours. Not only that, but exercise will give you a ton of energy and stamina over time. It takes energy to exercise, but as you continue exercising over days and weeks, you build endurance, which in turn gives you more energy on a daily basis, which makes it easier to exercise even more if you want, in another virtuous cycle. This stuff all feeds on itself, so your main concern is just to get the ball rolling. After that, there's a good chance it will pick up momentum all by itself. Pretty cool, huh?

I know that not everyone who looks in the mirror feels ready to just "up and get a gym membership." In fact—in the tradition of people who like to straighten up before the housecleaner arrives—I am definitely one of those people who wanted to "lose a little weight" before going to the gym.

Here's the good news: Exercise is definitely important, but it's less important than what you put into your mouth. After all of my years training, reading, learning, and teaching... I've come to the conclusion that about 65% of losing weight and having excellent health are the result of good diet and nutrition, with only about 35% going to exercise. What does this mean? It means that, when I want to lose weight, I make food consumption my main focus during the initial weight-loss period. Don't get me wrong... I still exercise. But if you want to lose, say, 10 pounds, it's a lot easier to do it through modest portion control and lots of green smoothies than it is through running on the treadmill. A *LOT* easier!

There are, of course, some people who get totally motivated by incorporating intense physical fitness right away and I love that! (Keep up the great work because you'll see results much faster if you do that.) But if you lack the motivation, focus primarily on diet first, with moderate exercise, and wait for the virtuous cycle to kick in. The moment you feel the urge to "step up" your fitness regimen, then pounce on it. You'll just know when it feels right. Some day, you'll wake up feeling great, noticing that you feel healthier and are closer to your target weight, and you'll say, "today I think I'll step things up a bit." And it won't be hard or kick your butt. It will be that your body has adapted.

To be considered truly healthy, you have to be fit. If you are slim, with little or no cellulite, clear glowing skin (this goes for men too!), but you can't make it up three flights of stairs without huffing and puffing, then, I'm sorry, but you are not truly healthy. We all know the amazing benefits of working out. The mental empowerment alone is worth the effort. Studies have shown that one of the best medicines for depression is exercise. My goal here is to offer you some ways to get started and to get that ever-important little jump-start that gets the momentum and motivation going. If you are like me and you do not feel like immediately going to the gym just yet, I have included ways for you to start incorporating exercise into your routine now, during your regular routine, even if it's only on a small scale. This gets the momentum building, and this gets you excited about exercise, thinking about it, used to the idea, and ultimately accustomed to the *habit* of exercise. I am a big believer in baby steps, so here are some tiny things to start doing today (if you are not already). They may seem obvious, but if you are not doing them... then... hhmmm... *WHAT THE HECK ARE YOU WAITING FOR?* (Be sure to check with your physician first.)

- Take the stairs instead of the elevator every chance you get. Even if you only have the stamina to walk up one flight and then take the elevator the rest. Do it. You will see your strength growing right away, giving you the energy to do more the next time.

- Park in a spot far away from the door to whichever establishment you are headed. This is probably the easiest way to get extra steps into your day. It's truly a no-brainer and if you are not doing it already, get to it!

- Take an 8-minute walk two times a day. That is the approximate length of two of your favorite songs. So, put on your headphones (keep them nearby you at all times) and listen to two of your favorite *get movin' tunes* and get out there and WALK! Or jog or whatever, but just move!

- Set a timer on your cell phone or watch to stand up and stretch every 3-4 hours (more is ideal, but I realize that baby steps are important. If you do it every three hours now, it will not be long until you are doing it every two hours). When you stretch, try to touch your toes, stretch your neck, pull your knee (one at a time) to your chest, reach to the ceiling, etc. Take nice long and deep breaths, while you are doing this. Very effective at helping your circulation and the all-important toxic-removing lymph system, which does its job primarily through *movement* of your body and limbs.

- Clean the house. This used to seem like a boring chore, but not if you realize that this is actually physical activity, too. While you're at it, put on some good music that makes you boogie a little extra while cleaning. Not only burn a few extra calories, but you'll also start to embed a habit of movement and energy in all that you do—not unlike children do. Remember, life is a party... so *DANCE!*

- Do yard work; in fact, learn to love it. This follows the same logic as cleaning the house. Yard work can definitely help you burn calories, so get out there and rake leaves, plant flowers, mow the lawn (not a riding mower), or shovel snow and call it a day because you just accomplished a lot (exercise and chores, simultaneously).

- Wear ankle weights around the house. My mom even wears hers to the store and people always comment that it's a great idea.

- Dance to your favorite music.

- Do sideways leg lifts, or calf raises, while you're blow drying your hair.

- Do three pushups a day (if you're new to this), or more (if you're not new). Not girly style either—no knees on the floor, if you can help it. Okay, if you need your knees on the floor, that's okay, you'll build up to the real deal version soon. If you can't do three pushups, then do one or two. You'll gain strength quickly, and you'll find yourself adding extra pushups all the time.

- Get a hula-hoop and do this during one of your favorite songs every day, for the duration of the whole song.

- If you live in a house or building with stairs, when you are watching TV at night, during every commercial break, take the opportunity to go up and down your stairs 3-4 times (with ankle weights on, if you have them). If you don't have stairs, then do abdominal crunches for one whole commercial, then do jumping jacks for the next whole commercial and so on and so forth.

- Get a jump rope. I cannot tell you enough how amazing jumping rope is. It's one of the highest calorie burning activities you can do and guess what? You burn a ton of calories *in a fraction of the time* you would spend walking, using the elliptical machine or stair-stepper at the gym, etc. It's that intense. In fact, I'll bet that most of you can't even jump rope for a minute straight (the style where you only jump off the ground once per rotation of the jump rope). Try it. It's fun, cheap, and can be done almost anywhere.

- Exercise in the morning. This really ensures that you do it and don't let "life get in the way." Then, if you have extra time at night, do something else physical (such as the suggestions found here) and it's added bonus calorie burning. Conveniently, I have a dog, and dogs need to pee. This forces me to step outside. And so often, while I'm at it—shoes on, leash on the dog—I'll say "what the heck" and take a walk around the block. Not only is it good for me, it's good for the dog, both his body and spirit. He would walk ten times a day if it were up to him, and there's a lesson in that for all of us. Before we were creatures of cars, phones, mortgages, and 9-to-5 servitude, we were creatures of walking, running, gathering food, playing. We are fundamentally... creatures of *movement*.

- Take a 10-minute walk after lunch and/or dinner. This helps facilitate digestion, too. Robert E. Thayer, Ph.D., a professor of biological psychology at California State University, found that as little as 10-minutes of brisk walking leads to very significant increases in energy.

- Take up a new hobby for spare time in the evening. This is when a lot of people feel restless, so find something to occupy your time other than just watching TV and snacking. Some great examples are yard work, gardening, playing with your pet or children, dance lessons, music lessons, or art, such as painting, pottery, woodworking, or making things out of stained glass.

- Posture! It's very important to stand up straight, sit up straight, and walk with excellent posture. Poor posture can reduce the amount of oxygen you take into your lungs... by more than *30 percent!* But that's not all, poor posture affects the way you feel mentally. It affects your mindset. According to Rene Cailliet, M.D., chairman of the department of physical medicine at the Santa Monica Hospital Center, when you're stooped over, you tend to feel old, even depressed sometimes. So, sit up straight, shoulders back and take a deep breath. This can make all the difference in the world!

- Breathe! This is one of the most simple and effective ways to increase your energy and prepare yourself for exercise. Follow these steps:

1. Inhale for a count of two

2. Hold your breath for four seconds

3. Exhale for a count of six

4. Increase these times as you're able

5. You can even do this in your car or at your desk while you're working.

- Stay hydrated. When you are eating a diet full of water rich fruits and vegetables, you will not need to drink as much water as you used to. However, more is better than less here, so I still drink plenty of water throughout the day. This is especially important when exercising, during the hotter summer months, or if you live in a dry climate. Drinking plenty of water helps keep me energized and alert. When I am looking for an extra little "oomphf" of energy, I drink ice water to wake me up, or I drink my favorite brand of water, called *metromint*® — which actually has mint flavoring! This stuff is exhilarating, refreshing, and just tastes fantastic. I love it!

One thing to keep in mind about water is that filtered tap water is just as healthy as bottled, costs much less, and is far better on the environment. It's best to buy bottled water only when there is no alternative. I sometimes even make my own version of mint water by adding a stem of mint leaves to my own water and letting it soak overnight. Delicious and so refreshing!

"Nothing great was ever achieved
without enthusiasm."

— Ralph Waldo Emerson

CHAPTER 7

RAW QUESTIONS

*"Nothing will benefit human health and increase
the chances for survival of life on Earth as much as
the evolution to a vegetarian diet."*

— Albert Einstein

COMMON QUESTIONS REGARDING THE RAW LIFESTYLE

Is Raw Expensive?

No, living the Raw lifestyle is not expensive. In the beginning stages, it can *seem* expensive, but in the long run it is definitely not. Keep the following in mind:

1. During the beginning period, when you are new to Raw, you're trying a lot of new recipes and you typically don't have all of the ingredients on hand, so you're frequently buying new ingredients as you stock up your pantry. Once you're stocked up with all the appropriate seasonings, herbs and ingredients (things like Raw agave nectar, Raw chocolate, Raw carob, etc) then you will only purchase them from time to time.

2. Living the Raw lifestyle means not eating out at restaurants very often. This alone can save you a lot of

money. In fact, if you currently eat out frequently, you could save hundreds of dollars each month.

3. The equipment cost you pay in the beginning can add up, but just remember you probably won't need to buy these items again (or for a very long time) if you purchase high quality equipment, so consider that when you are shopping—buy for quality, not the best price. That said, if you can't afford it, you do not have to pay a lot of money for your kitchen equipment when you are just beginning. Reasonably good equipment is available at good prices, so don't let money stop you. Use what you have or buy what you can afford. Later on, you can start equipping your kitchen with higher quality kitchen tools to facilitate the Raw lifestyle. Ask for these gifts for holidays, birthdays, anniversaries, etc. Later in this book, I will tell you, in order of importance, the best products to buy to set up your Raw kitchen.

4. Remember the things you will not be buying, which will save you money. Meat is expensive. Supplements are VERY expensive—most (if not all) will no longer be necessary. Processed and packaged food is expensive. Going to restaurants is expensive. Doctor co-pays and bills are expensive. Prescription drugs are expensive. Being sick and staying home from work is expensive. Not having enough energy to really pay attention to your kids and be there for them 100% is expensive.

5. For some people, the transition to Raw can be challenging (cravings for cooked food, pressure from outsiders, advertising galore about the deadly but addictive foods that have made obesity an epidemic in this country). At times, it may almost feel as if you are

depriving yourself, or that you're on a "diet" as opposed to living a "lifestyle." To compensate for the mental anguish some people experience, they find themselves trying all kinds of Raw stuff, including elaborate and rich recipes (all varied and all needing different ingredients, of course), exotic "super" foods, books, videos, etc. It is almost as if people do this to keep their decision justified, or their minds focused, "on a mission," or preoccupied, to help facilitate their wide-sweeping change in lifestyle. Additionally, you may find yourself making all kinds of food for others to sample (in getting them to understand and support you, or maybe just trying to impress them, or even encouraging them to try the lifestyle for themselves). It's all perfectly natural, but keep in mind that these—exotic foods, learning materials, parties, etc.—can increase the financial cost of going Raw.

No Hot Food? Not Even in the Winter?

A common question asked of me is "How does one stay warm in a cold climate, while living the Raw lifestyle?"

People live the Raw lifestyle all over the world, in all climates and it's quite simple. Here are a couple of things you can do to help:

- Warm your food in a dehydrator. Simply place your food for 1-2 hours in a dehydrator set at 130-140 degrees (see Chapter 13 for details).

- Use warming spices like cayenne pepper, ginger, garlic, etc.

- Warm your soup or sauce a little on the stove, but only to a temperature that you can still put your finger in it and keep it there. Or put it in a warm water bath.

- Eat and drink foods at room temperature. For foods stored in the fridge, take them out in advance to warm up to room temperature before eating.

- Exercise! One of the best and most efficient ways to get your blood circulating is through physical activity.

- Drink warm herbal tea. It's not Raw, but if it helps warm you up, then it's worth it, and this is not bad for you in the way that it's bad to destroy your food's nutritional content through cooking.

- Keep in mind that after your body cleanses and you have detoxed, you probably won't have as much trouble keeping warm because your circulation will have improved.

- Dress warmer. Obvious? It works!

Will There Be Variety Living the Raw Lifestyle?

Emphatically, YES! Having variety in your diet is important so that you don't get bored. Remember, *"variety is the spice of life."* Getting variety with a Raw plant-based diet can be as easy as using different produce seasonally, weekly, and even daily. I find that most people crave variety (especially in the beginning stages of going Raw) because they are used to variety in their previous diets, and because their minds need it in order to stay motivated and disciplined. The big need for variety tends to actually decrease over time. That might not help you in this moment right now though. So, what will help right now is that

Raw food comes in many different, amazing dishes, from lasagna, to veggie burgers, to granola, to nut milk, to burritos, pizza, and more. Furthermore, Raw food has global flair. You can enjoy Mexican, Italian, Asian, and Caribbean flavors, to name just a few.

Should I Take Supplements?

I generally do not use supplements and I do not feel the need to recommend supplements to people who eat a well-balanced, primarily Raw organic diet (with "primarily" meaning that 70% or more of your diet comprises Raw, organic, plant-based food). Think of the money you will save by not purchasing supplements anymore! There are times, however, that supplementation can be a good idea:

- I believe that people who are still eating a lot of cooked food could benefit from taking an enzyme supplement. But, please keep in mind, this will never replace the potential health benefits of eating a mostly Raw diet. I only recommend enzyme supplementation during your transition period, or when circumstances prevent you from having access to Raw foods.

- When traveling abroad, it might be important to bring supplements such as probiotics, enzymes, as well as something such as Raw camu-camu wild berry powder, which has a very high concentration of vitamin C (available at NaturalZing.com). I also always bring a green powder supplement (my favorite is Vitamineral Green). This way, you continue to get plenty of greens in your diet while traveling. For details and recommendations, see KristensRaw.com/store.

- B-12 is a special case (see below).

Will I Become B12 Deficient?

Because plants don't produce vitamin B12, the uninformed commonly suggest meat as a source of the vitamin. However, B12 is actually not a chemical compound, it's a microbe — a bacteria that thrives in soil. Animal flesh is therefore not an original source of the vitamin. B12 is co-incidentally found in beef because it also thrives in the digestive tracts of cattle. Pre-industrial humans received more than adequate amounts of B12 in small amounts of soil consumed on unwashed vegetables (we don't need very much). Today, our vegetables are usually washed before we eat, meaning vegans need to make sure they are absorbing adequate amounts of B12.

But the key word is "absorbing." According to Marieb's Human Anatomy and Physiology, vitamin B12 can be destroyed by highly alkaline and highly acid conditions. This means that much of the B12 in meat would easily be destroyed by the high levels of hydrochloric acid produced by our stomachs during the digestion of meat. This may explain why meat-eaters are statistically just as likely to have a B12 deficiency as vegans, even though their diet contains more of the vitamin. Also, for meat-eaters, as a result of modern factory farming techniques, there are antibiotics contained in meat that are lethal to the vitamin B12 microbe. Gabriel Cousens, M.D., argues that vitamin B12 deficiency is typically caused by lack of absorption in the intestinal tract rather than a lack of this vitamin in the diet.

Improve your digestion and you will improve your absorption of vitamin B12. I recommend that you get your B12 levels checked with a simple blood test annually. If it turns out that your levels are low, then supplement. I have been vegan for over five years and I have my B12 levels checked once a year. I have never been deficient, but if my levels were ever to approach the low end of the recommended range, then I would supplement as needed.

There are a variety of B12 supplements available at your local health food store or from NaturalZing.com.

Should I Eat Sea Vegetables?

Sea veggies can contribute a lot to a Raw/living foods diet: minerals, enzymes, vitamins, protein, fiber, and marine phytochemicals. Sea vegetables contain significant amounts of vitamins, especially the B vitamins. A serving of dulse (about 7g, 1/3 cup) provides about 10% RDA Vitamin B-2 (Riboflavin) and about 42% RDA Vitamin B-6. You can find sea veggies at health food stores and on the Internet. Some people add sea veggies (dulse, kelp, etc.) to soups, smoothies, and salads or they use nori sheets to make the popular nori veggie rolls.

What If I NEED Chocolate!?

No problem! Eat Raw chocolate, better known in the Raw Food world as "Cacao Beans and Nibs." Some say, and I agree, "Raw chocolate is the new red wine." And why shouldn't it be? Studies show Raw chocolate as being the number one source of magnesium, as well as the number one source of antioxidants of any whole food. David Wolfe, one of the biggest proponents of Raw chocolate, believes that Raw chocolate can naturally decrease your appetite and increase your energy. He also claims that Raw chocolate contains less than 1/20th the amount of caffeine found in an equivalent amount of coffee. It also contains phenylethylamine (PEA) — this is what our brains secrete when we fall in love. Need I say more?

You can eat the Cacao Beans and Nibs straight up (although they are bitter by themselves), add them to Raw trail mix, or you can grind them into a powder and mix it agave nectar or Raw almond butter (divine!). You can also add Raw chocolate to your smoothies. My favorite form of Raw chocolate is to get it in the powder form, available on my website at KristensRaw.com/store.

This powder is extremely airy and light. It blends perfectly and has the richest, most chocolaty taste ever. For recipes, see my blog at KristensRaw.com.

What If I'm Addicted to Caffeine?

No problem! Been there, done that, when it comes to caffeine. I can definitely write on the subject. There are a variety of ways to deal with being addicted to caffeine and getting off it. Try any or all of the following suggestions:

- Hot peppers can work wonders for your overall health and caffeine addiction. For the hard-core folks out there, think habanera peppers. If you find those too hot, then start with a mild red pepper and work your way up. The idea here is that it must be hot enough to release endorphins—the brain's mechanism for dulling pain. The endorphins tackle two issues for you: 1) providing energy so you don't miss the caffeine and 2) fighting headaches that may result from caffeine withdrawal.

- Drink daily green juices, including wheat grass if you like, which will help alkalize your blood and reduce cravings for coffee and caffeine. Add carrot juice to the mix, either straight or in the green juice.

- Drink fresh squeezed orange juice in the morning to give yourself some pure Raw energy instead of stimulated energy from caffeine.

- To help avoid severe withdrawal problems, consider migrating off gradually. You can start with half decaf (or just make the regular caffeine version with fewer coffee beans when you're making it at home. You can work your way to 100% decaf and/or green tea, then to herbal tea.

morning and between meals. It is true that you tend to drink less water when eating a Raw diet because you are getting plenty of water in your foods, as opposed to cooking it out. (All that steam you see coming off of a hot cooked meal is the water your body is supposed to be getting from food itself, just like every other animal on the planet). A good rule of thumb is to take notice of your urine. It should be very pale in color (almost clear in many cases and quite odorless). If your urine is bright or dark yellow, then you should drink more water.

What's All This I Hear About Green Smoothies? Are They Really That Good For Me?

Green smoothies are a wonderful addition to anyone's lifestyle. I can't emphasize this enough. They are a great way to start eating cleaner and getting tons of energy right away. Greens are full of many different nutrients, vitamins and minerals. The problem with eating greens (especially dark greens) is that they don't always taste the best (they can be quite bitter). But, that's not a problem anymore, because with green smoothies, which add ingredients that reduce the bitterness, they taste delicious. In fact, kids love them, too! They get excited about drinking something that is "green" and it makes it fun... I like to come up with fun names to make them even more exciting for children (okay, and more fun for *me!*).

Many people use green energy smoothies to help lose weight, because they help reduce cravings and can replace meals and/or snacks. Green smoothies are extremely satiating and filling because they're loaded with plenty of fiber, nutrients and minerals. Not only that, green smoothies can help reduce cholesterol and steady blood sugar levels. And, if you're having a sweet tooth, drink one of these first, before indulging in something less healthy. You'll be amazed at how much it reduces your craving for sweets. As my mom always said, "They take the edge off" of cravings. They're also great for weight loss if you drink one of these 30-60 minutes before you have a meal. I like to think of it as an appetite suppressant... but a healthy one! This way I don't overeat at meals if I come to the dinner table and I'm not famished, ready to wolf down everything in sight.

Green Smoothies are terrific for traveling or when you are running errands. I make sure I always have a Green Smoothie with me. I'll take it to the movies for my snack (hidden in my purse—sshhhh... don't tell the movie police). When I'm out running errands for the day, I keep one or two of these in a cooler in my car. This way, if I get hungry or have any cravings, I can drink my green smoothie, be satisfied and full of pure, natural energy. They are so good! As I'm writing this, I'm thinking up what kind I am going to make today!

When deciding what to put into your Green Smoothie, consider the following greens: spinach, parsley, kale, swiss chard, celery, arugula, sprouts, cilantro, celery, romaine lettuce. These are a great source of quality protein and minerals.

Make one and see for yourself. It's super easy.

Basic Organic Green Smoothie Recipe

> 1-2 cups filtered or spring water
> 1 handful (or more) of organic leafy greens
> 2 pieces (or more) of organic fruit

Put all of it in a blender and give it a whirl. It should taste really good; if it tastes too "green," simply add more fruit (or use fewer greens next time). You'll find yourself adding more greens over time because your tastes adjust and your body loves getting the greens, so you end up craving them.

Variations

Herbs

Herbs are full of nutrition and pack tons of flavor. Make a smoothie with a couple pieces of fruit and 1-2 tablespoons of fresh herbs (mince them beforehand so they blend well). See my blog for recipes and more information: KristensRaw.com.

Organic Edible Flowers

These make a lovely addition to a smoothie and these, too, pack some fabulous nutrition. See my blog for a recipe and more information: KristensRaw.com.

Stevia

Stevia is a great sweetener option for green smoothies when you want to use less fruit. Fresh stevia leaves are the best, but if you don't have that available, you can find stevia in your local health food store. It's available in liquid form, white powder, or green powder forms. If I can't get it fresh, I try to buy the green powder version because it's the least processed of the options. Check the bulk food section of the store where they sell bulk herbs and spices.

Extracts and Flavorings

Add 1/2 - 1 teaspoon of vanilla extract (or any flavor extract) or cinnamon, nutmeg, etc., to make your smoothie more interesting and fun.

There are so many variations that you can do with your fresh green smoothies that I promise you couldn't possibly ever get bored. I have a number of great smoothie recipes in my book, *Kristen Suzanne's EASY Raw Vegan Smoothies, Juices, Elixirs and Drinks*, so be sure and check that out (KristensRaw.com).

The Infamous Salt Question... What Kind Do I Use?

All life on earth began in the oceans, so it's no surprise that organisms' cellular fluids chemically resemble sea water. Saltwater in the ocean is "salty" due to many, many minerals, not just sodium chloride (table salt). We need these minerals, not coincidentally, in roughly the same proportion that they exist in... guess where?... the ocean! (You've just gotta love Mother Nature.)

So when preparing food, I always use sea salt, which you can buy at any health food store. Better still is sea salt that was deposited into salt beds before the industrial revolution started spewing toxins into the world's waterways... like a million years ago. My personal preference is Himalayan Crystal Salt, fine granules. It's mined high in the mountains from ancient sea-beds, has a beautiful pink color, and imparts more than 84 essential minerals into your diet. You can use either the Himalayan crystal variety or Celtic Sea Salt, but I would highly recommend sticking to at least one of these two. You can find links to buy Himalayan crystal salt at KristensRaw.com/store.

RAW VERSUS NOT RAW

Here are a few items that might confuse people as to whether they are Raw or not.

Sprouted Bread

There are some "sprouted" breads currently available in health food stores. These are probably not Raw. The research I did showed that most are heated at temperatures around 200 degrees or more. If you are not sure, I would research by calling the company's number on the package. Alternatively, you can make your own Raw sprouted bread.

Tofu

Tofu is not Raw. You can, however, find sprouted soy beans in many health food stores.

Bulgur Wheat

This is commonly used in conventional tabouli recipes. Bulgur wheat is not Raw.

Corn on the Cob

Yes, you can eat this raw, right off the cob.

Rice Wraps

These are not Raw. However, they can be used by someone new to Raw. Even though they are not Raw, you can fill them with a bunch of delicious Raw veggies and sauce during your transition period.

Lentils, Beans, Grains

There are a variety of sprouted lentils, beans and grains that you can eat. Many of them are available already sprouted and ready-to-eat in health food stores. Avoid unsprouted lentils, unsprouted dry beans, and unsprouted grains.

Potatoes

I don't recommend eating uncooked white potatoes. They are too hard on your digestive system.

A good rule of thumb is this: Foods that need to be cooked to make them digestible, palatable, or "safe to eat" should be minimized in your diet.

Because heating starches (when required to make them more digestible) destroys nutrients, eating starchy foods is not ideal and can leave you malnourished. Alternatively, if you eat enough of these to get sufficient nutrition, then you consume too many calories.

CHAPTER 8

CRAVINGS

You may be surprised to learn that cooked food can be *highly addictive.* But the more you *know,* and the more you read over time, the more confident and empowered you will feel about your choice to live the Raw lifestyle. We are bombarded with advertising every minute of the day for processed, cooked, unhealthy and addictive foods. We need this Raw Armor of knowledge to shield ourselves and stand tall, saying *"no"* to unhealthy food and cravings.

> *"The pain of discipline is much easier than the pain of regret."*
>
> — Jim Rohn

DON'T WORRY... IT'S NOT GOING ANYWHERE

Here is a great trick... one thing to always remember if you are craving a certain food is that "it is not going anywhere." It was not that long ago that our ancestors were barely scraping out a living, just trying to find enough food to survive. Before agriculture, food availability was irregular, and our bodies were well adapted to this with the ability to convert extra food into fat that would carry us through hard times, such as every winter. That was good back then, but it works against us now. Our natural instincts tell us to eat eat eat. But our society has managed to eliminate those times of scarcity. This is a recipe for obesity!

Among other things, cravings are the body's way of telling you to store food "in case you run out." (And the effect is even worse for people who grew up in a large family!).

So one of the best things you can tell yourself the next time you're experiencing a craving, is that the food isn't going anywhere. It will always be there later if you want it. This will help relax your mindset and enable you to step back and take a look at the bigger picture. Trust me, this really works, even if you have to say the words out loud: "I can always have this later if I want."

Here is an exercise that is very effective: Write down the following questions and carry them with you everywhere. The next time you want to go off the Raw lifestyle and give in to a craving, take a moment to reflect on the questions. Even if it's while you're in line to buy whatever it is you "think" you need at that moment.

DO I REALLY WANT THIS?

Maybe I do. But, should I have it? If so, why? Do I have to have it now? How would I feel if I came back later tonight or even tomorrow? Would I still want it? If so, why don't I try that? Realize that it is not going anywhere (Taco Bell, Starbucks, popcorn at the movies, whatever it is) and I can have it at a later date. Just tell myself "no" for now.

I was amazed at how many times I was COMFORTABLE with saying "no" to myself in that moment because I knew I could have it later, *if* I even wanted it later. I was comfortable and it worked. What's even better is that it was a very rare occasion that I even went back for it at a later time. I was so empowered at having said "no" to an addiction. For example, we all went to Starbucks once as a group of friends and I thought, "Well, I really want this. I'm tired and I want the caffeine and I need the energy because I have a lot of work to do tonight." BUT,

I did my little exercise above. I acknowledged to myself that I did want and need it, but that I was willing to wait. Starbucks is open until 10:30pm near me. I told myself to pass at that moment, go home, start working and if I still wanted it later on, I'd get in the car and go. I was so empowered and felt awesome standing in the face of my addiction and saying "nah, I'll pass." Well, guess what? Not only did I not crave it once I was home, but, I didn't want to get back in my car and drive to Starbucks anyway. It became more of a "to-do" and I just passed on the whole thing.

It always helps to make the object of your craving inconvenient to access.

The more times you do this, the stronger your mind gets and the less addicted you are because you're not putting those substances back in your body that you'll end up having to deal with at a later date. Success begets success and eventually, discipline isn't required because it will be your habit.

BEING PREPARED

There might be times when you're craving a certain food. When those times come upon you, be prepared. Studies show that cravings are often fleeting and go as quickly as they come. In reality, they tend to go away in as little as 5-minutes. One way to ensure this is to immediately distract yourself by doing "something"... anything. Usually within 5-minutes, the craving is gone. Jumping rope for a couple of minutes is a great example.

THE CRAVING REPLACEMENT CHART

Here is a list of foods to try so you do not indulge in the actual craving. If you crave the item on the left, then replace it with the item or choices on the right:

TYPICAL CRAVING   RAW REPLACEMENT

TYPICAL CRAVING	RAW REPLACEMENT
Chocolate	Raw chocolate
Caramel	Raw carob
Dessert	Dates stuffed with pecans
Sugar	Fruit smoothie
Ice cream	Raw ice cream
Jello or fruit-flavored candy	Fruit Smoothie, fruit, dates
Milk	Raw nut/seed milk
Milkshake	Raw nut/seed milk with crushed ice or frozen banana
Protein shake supplement	Raw tahini milk or hemp shake
Pastry	Raw granola
Meat, rice, beans	Raw pate, hummus with veggies, flax bread with cheese spread, or Raw marinated mushrooms
Pizza	Raw pizza

Italian food	Raw Italian food:
	  - *Pasta*
	  - *Lasagna*

Fish and sushi	Nori rolls, sea vegetables
Mashed potatoes	Raw mashed potatoes
Cheese	Raw nut/seed cheese
Cheese	Nutritional yeast and water
Chips and dip	Raw hummus, ranch dip, dehydrated zucchini chips
Mexican food	Raw Mexican pate

Caffeine, drugs, alcohol	"Plant Blood," a.k.a.:
	  - *Fresh green juice*
	  - *Fresh carrot juice*
	  - *Fress apple juice*
	  - *Fresh orange juice*

CHAPTER 9

SETTING YOURSELF UP TO WIN

I am going to share with you the best ideas and ways to easily start living the Raw lifestyle and stay with it. You are going to learn everything you need to know in order to set yourself up to win. It's easy once you know how. Let's go!

IMPORTANT NOTE: Many people have no problems whatsoever jumping quickly and completely into Raw and never looking back. It happens all the time, in fact. If that's you, then you're in great shape and the tips in this chapter may be totally unnecessary, or something to consider only in time of duress, such as holidays or the occasional cravings crisis. But for anybody who has ever struggled with self-control, especially when it comes to food, then these tips—some of which are pretty unconventional—will give you great weapons in your arsenal, and lots of fun at the same time.

KNOW YOUR OUTCOME

Knowing your outcome is one of the most important things you can do for yourself, so let's begin by envisioning what you want to look and feel like. Close your eyes for a moment and just think about this. Feel it. Pretend you had a magic wand... what would you do with it? What kinds of things would you change about yourself, your health, your body, your energy? Think about how you will feel when you are at your desired weight. Think about how you will feel with tons of energy. What are some of the things you're going to do with all that energy? What are some of the clothes you're going to wear with your new body?

Remember these visions. Keep them at the front of your mind. One way to do this is to spend part of your time in the shower thinking about these visions. It's the perfect setting—you're not distracted and it's the first thing you do each day.

Visions transform into goals when you commit them to paper. Write down your goals on post-it notes and stick them everywhere so they are always in your face... always reminding you of the new "you" that you are becoming and the new "lifestyle" that you're living. This is how you *support yourself* because you will not always have a cheerleading squad pumping you up and cheering you on. When I first realized this, I simply started pumping myself up and became my own cheerleader. And, these are the things I did to support myself. They're just small little notes for me. I wrote notes and reminders such as:

"Eat 100% Raw for three days straight"

"My Law Is Raw"

"Do something Physical every day"

"Do 10 pushups"

"I have clear, glowing skin"

"Kristen, you rock!"

"I can feel the energy coursing through my body!"

"Kristen, visualize your success and your healthy body"

I placed these notes all over the place: the refrigerator, car dashboard, computer, desk, bathroom mirror, nightstand, even in my purse and makeup bag. Then, every time I looked at these I was reminded of my lifestyle and future accomplishments. It becomes very empowering because it's always on your mind.

Typically, what happens, depending on the note, is that you end up doing what you wrote down *right at that moment.* Sometimes you do it every time you see it (especially if it's a physical activity like doing a few pushups or jumping jacks). Or, you end up envisioning your goal and success every time you see the note, attracting the goal to yourself faster than ever.

Always ask yourself in everything you do... "What is the outcome I want to result from this activity." I try do this for everything so that it becomes a habit. Even when I'm brushing my teeth, I think to myself, "I really want to get a thorough brushing so that I prevent cavities." Or, when I'm preparing food for my clients, I think to myself, "I envision my clients loving my food so much, feeling wonderful after they eat it... that is the outcome I'm after." Or, when I'm visiting my mom, I think to myself, "I want my mom to have fun and know how much I love her." And, I think about this on my drive over to her house. I used to have "know my outcome" written and taped to my kitchen cupboard and in my car to serve as a reminder to think about that in everything I did, and every time I was driving somewhere. Now it's second nature and I automatically think about this all day long. I used to have to remind myself with positive notes, but now I just remember. So, you can see that you only keep these notes up temporarily and then you swap them out with new notes as you progress.

BLOGGING: THE NEW JOURNALING

If I were writing this two years ago, I would implore you to begin keeping a daily journal that tracks what you eat, how you're *moving* (exercising), and what you're thinking about with respect to these, if not all aspects of your life. (For those of you who don't know what blogging is, it means keeping an online journal, which other people can read, and if you allow them to, they can post follow-up messages. More on this, and how to set up a blog, in a moment.)

Journaling still has its place—especially for private thoughts—but I now find blogging to be much, MUCH more effective, for one main reason: feedback.

Unlike a journal, when you blog, you tell the world. If you like, you can be anonymous, by using a screen name or "handle" instead of your real name. Both real names and fictitious names are extremely common; it's a matter of personal preference (many people have one or more of each and talk about different things using different names, such as professional matters under their real name, and, say, politics or sports under a pseudonym like "sportsfan057.")

When you tell the world, several important things happen:

Again, you get feedback. The most common form of feedback will be people leaving comments and questions on your blog. You can set it up so that the public either can or can't view the comments, or they can view them only after you've first approved the messages.

You meet people—sometimes people will contact you directly via email. (You can still maintain your anonymity if you like, by using a different email address.) Because they're contacting you based on what you've written, their emails are frequently very relevant to the subject matter and what you're trying to do with Raw. They may have questions they'd like to ask you, answers for questions that you've posed, suggestions you never would have thought of on your own, or they might just write to say "hi."

When you blog, you provide knowledge to others who may follow in your footsteps, tomorrow or ten years from now. What you write might be archived and searchable for years—or even *decades!*—to come. In most endeavors in life, somebody else has already been there. Any problem you encounter, somebody else has already encountered... and solved. The collective wisdom of millions of people recording their experiences has immeasurable value to others.

But here is the SINGLE MOST important reason to maintain a blog instead of a journal...

You're much more likely to stick with it. Perhaps a hundred times more likely, for one simple reason: again, you get feedback. When you write something, your natural curiosity will start nagging at you, wondering whether anybody has left any comments. This curiosity alone reinforces the behavior. But when somebody actually writes something, especially something very reinforcing... look out! You'll be so motivated to write more, you won't believe it.

To set up your blog, just go to Blogspot.com and create an account just as I did. It's easy and free. You can see my blog at KristensRaw.blogspot.com.

Don't worry if you don't get feedback right away. Just keep writing. Eventually people will find your blog, especially if it's about Raw food, as there is quite an active Raw food community online, and people are eager to search and reach out to one another. Start by going to other people's Raw food blogs on Blogspot.com and leaving comments, questions, and words of encouragement for them. This is a great way for people to find out about your blog (there will be a link to your blog when you post a message on their blog).

Keeping a blog about Raw food and/or your life is one of the most rewarding things you can do. Once you start, you become addicted to it (in a good way). As you look back on it, you'll read it with pride, self-discovery, and fun.

To start, keep track of every little success you have. You build on success, and this is how you reinforce your progress.

Keeping track of everything is the best way to measure your success. This is critical for making the journey (and life in general) fun, rewarding, and motivating. Every time you look back and see progress, no matter how small, you'll be inspired to do more. Even if you are just starting out, writing things like "I ate Raw food for breakfast, I walked up and down my stairs two times" then later that day you write, "I ate mostly Raw at lunch..." This might sound simple, or too boring to blog about, but it's very important—it's tracking your progress and demonstrating to the world that people *actually do live this way.* When you look at it the following day, you'll know the next step you need to take to get to the next level.

Often, you'll get an idea in a flash when you're away from your computer. This is very common... you want to blog about the idea and you don't want to forget it. So go out and get yourself a special blogging notebook just for this purpose. I went out and bought special pens of a few different colors. I got stickers for fun and to add zest. I don't hold any punches when it comes to my notebook... the paper is colored, the pens are colored (some even have glitter ink) and my gusto with stickers would put Japanese schoolgirls to shame.

Keep your notebook with you everywhere you go. Keep it by your bed at night, on the bathroom counter while you get ready in the morning, by your computer throughout the day, in your car where ever you go. Then, when have a thought you can quickly and easily jot it down.

If you miss a day or two of posting to your blog, don't sweat it. Don't worry about playing catch-up and backtracking on the days you missed, just pick up where you are.

In my notebook, I write down and track the food I ate for the day. I write down when I'm wanting a cup of coffee or craving something cooked and how I'm going to quash the craving. I write down the physical activity I did for the day. Sometimes I record my weight, or my feelings, or my goals for the day or week or month.

Then, when I sit down to post something to my blog, I always have material. It's very easy and lots of fun.

Your notebook can become a journal of sorts, for keeping track of things whether you blog about them or not. This is a good place to list goals, for instance. I have a section in my notebook for all of my health goals. My original list looked like this:

My Ultimate Health Goals:

- Unlimited energy

- Get off all medications

- Eliminate addiction to caffeine

- Sleep better

- No headaches

- Empowered eating choices

- Weigh 123 pounds

- Rockin' lean n' fit body

- Cardio 4 times a week

- Lift weights 3-5 times a week

- Clear glowing skin

- Excellent mindset and memory

- 100% organic food at home

- Walk dog 4-5 times a week

- Ride bike 1 time a week...

LIST THEM ALL! Over time, you will have new goals to add and old ones to cross off.

It's important to look at these at least once a day, or as I like to say: *"KEEP THEM IN YOUR FACE."*

"In your face" means doing whatever it takes to make them impossible to miss. For instance, make copies of the list, put them all over your house, decorate them with colored pens, stickers, inspiring photos from magazines... whatever it takes.

I have my list of health goals typed and posted in different parts of my house, along with some inspiring quotes. I even change out the paper and put it on a different color every month. I literally schedule this on my calendar so I don't forget to do it! If the same sheet is there all the time, you get used to it being there and you might find yourself tuning it out, not paying attention to it anymore.

The way you handle this is by rewriting the list, maybe switching their order, using a different color ink or use a different color of paper. Cut it out into a different shape. Anything that changes the look of it and re-hang it everywhere, maybe in new places, like right next to the television. This way if there is an advertisement for some unhealthy, cooked food, you won't think about wanting it because you'll see all your awesome health goals posted right there. And, don't care how it looks to other people! This is what inspires others. Watch and you will see them doing the same thing after they learn from you.

TAKE PICTURES!

One of the best pieces of advice I can give is to take tons of pictures. Take them all the time! Post them to your blog. The reason taking pictures works is right in line with setting yourself up to win and blogging. It continuously reminds and inspires you to stay on this path. Take pictures of your counter tops being full of fresh organic produce. Have someone take pictures of you preparing Raw food in your kitchen. Take pictures of your new appliances. Take a picture to celebrate the cleaning out of your cupboards, when you throw away the junk food. It's a great reminder so you don't buy that unhealthy food again. Take pictures of your body as you get healthier and healthier. Tape some of the pictures into your notebook, onto your kitchen cupboards, the fridge door, your bathroom mirror—even inside your car, for a reminder and motivation the next time you're buying produce or resisting a craving for whatever unhealthy food establishment you happen to be passing by. Seriously, make it easy on yourself and do all the things I am suggesting in this book. They're fun and you will really enjoy yourself. If you truly want to succeed with this Raw lifestyle easily and while having a really fun time, then do these things.

And by all means, send me your success stories!

Kristen@KristensRaw.com

SCHEDULE REWARDS IN ADVANCE

Here's an item for your Raw notebook: a reward list.

Having a list of rewards that you can look forward to and experience is another great way to set yourself up for victory. This part is really fun! Write all the things you want and desire in your notebook. Even if you can't afford these rewards right now, or don't have the time, still write down everything because it is fun. Once you put something on paper, even if it is listed as a "reward" in your mind, it actually is a "goal," too. And, you probably know by now that goals on paper start to have a life of their own and you start moving toward the achievement of them automatically... just from writing them down.

The next great tip is to actually schedule some of your rewards... *in advance*. This creates a sense of accountability for yourself. If you want a massage really badly, and you need to earn it by being 100% Raw for two weeks straight, then call the spa and schedule it. Write it in your journal and write it on your calendar so you're constantly reminded of the reward.

Supporting and rewarding yourself for all wins, big and small, is crucial. This keeps you motivated. This keeps you smiling and unstoppable. In the beginning, when I began my Raw journey, I rewarded myself as much as possible. Every three days that I went 100% Raw, I treated myself to something in beauty or makeup or music or books and magazines (things that I love). Other ideas for rewards could be a great kitchen appliance, a Raw specialty food item (truffle oil or Raw chocolate), some new bath oils or soy candles. It's not that I had money coming out of my ears, but it was amazing because I only ended up doing it a few times... and even small, inexpensive items can make wonderfully satisfying symbolic rewards. After about four times of successfully sticking with 100% Raw for three-days, I was on a roll and I decided to up the ante by attempting to go for seven days straight, and then two weeks, a month, and so on.

There also came a time when I knew I could—if I wanted to—make my reward a cooked vegan meal (this was a "mental reward" for me). Some purists might not like that or agree with the philosophy behind it, but you have to do whatever works best for you, and this was something that worked for me... provided I didn't let it get out of control.

This self-control was the critical factor, which a lot of people find challenging. Cooked food is dangerously addictive, so I had to set myself up to win if I did this. One of the ways I ensured this is to never buy anything in the store that was for cooking. After all, my microwave, stove, and oven were out of commission because they are used for storage anyway—even my stovetop is covered in glass, with many small bottles of spices stacked on top. What a pain that would be to have to pull everything out just to use it for a few minutes... a technique not unlike shopping addicts who put their credit cards in a Ziploc bag, place it in a bowl of water and then stick it in the freezer, to be chipped out only in a financial emergency. Similarly, using your oven and microwave for storage makes it inconvenient to cook food. And not keeping ingredients for cooked food in your house helps you avoid temptation. It's these little tricks that keep you on track and accelerate your path to living the healthiest life possible. Keep in mind, this is generally important only during your transition to Raw; there will come a time when you won't be tempted even if these foods are in your house.

Keep in mind that if you use your mental reward for something that is not plant-based, you run the risk of feeling really sick after the reward. Your new healthy body can only handle so much, so don't over-do it by eating too much at one sitting or by eating junk. With a little sensible moderation, you don't have to "recover" after your reward, which wouldn't really be a reward then, would it? Don't reward yourself with something that will harm you. Personally, I don't feel that low-fat, vegan, cooked food is unhealthy if eaten occasionally. It's the *habit* that matters here, not the rare exception. Plus, these served not only as a meal for my physical body; these are mental rewards for me, which can do wonders for the spirit.

It might seem counter-intuitive to reward your physical efforts with something that doesn't seem to optimally support you physically, but you see, here is where I'm a little different than many hard-core Raw fooders out there. I'm aware that mental rewards are critical to success. Giving myself something that was cooked vegan (maybe a decaf soy cappuccino or perhaps steamed tofu and vegetables) was a relief and so much fun that to reward myself mentally was worth the price of the discipline it took to earn it.

This isn't the solution for everyone. I have clients that just can't get off the Raw path at all or they run the risk of falling off completely and going out of control with cooked food. Or, maybe you just want to be 100% Raw because that is your plan and goal. That is great because you'll be eating only the healthiest food in the world. If this is you, then you'll want to find other ways to reward yourself.

Maybe it's taking time for yourself to do the things that you like to do. Maybe it's buying a magazine or treating yourself to an activity that you would not normally do, like spending a weekend at a resort or going on a hot air balloon ride. Or taking a day off work and going to see a movie you've been dying to see. It doesn't matter what it is, just make sure you give yourself something to look forward to and give yourself timelines to do it by. Schedule them. If you feel like you are struggling during any point of the journey, all you have to do is look forward to the reward you're going to give yourself.

Some people might say, "Well, you shouldn't have to reward yourself. Your health should be the reward itself." Yes, this is fine and true for some... but, in the beginning stages, I am here to tell you, in those borderline cases where your strength is put to the test, when this is all new to you and you find yourself at home, too tired to make something Raw and you just want to go through the Taco Bell drive-through, these little rewards can make all the difference in the world.

When I was a kid, my mom used to reward us with money for good grades. Back then, I did not necessarily grasp the degree to which doing well in school had its own inherent long-term rewards. In fact, I don't know any kids who do, especially the young ones. However, knowing that I had a short-term reward coming for my efforts made learning more fun. Then, as if by magic, as I grew, I had more appreciation for being smart and I no longer needed the bribe (reward) because, by then, the good behavior was familiar, easy, natural, and an ingrained habit... one that I did with little thought, because it had become my normal way of doing things.

The same principle applies with anything new in your lifestyle, especially something that isn't part of mainstream society, such as Raw. Giving yourself great rewards in the beginning helps reinforce the behavior of eating Raw. In the beginning, while you are getting used to handling different social situations and learning how to set yourself up to be successful at it (and if you're going through detox) then you really benefit from a few simple rewards, and maybe one BIG reward when you reach a major milestone.

AVOIDING ROUTINE TEMPTATION

In setting yourself up for victory, it will be much easier if you simply *avoid* foods that tempt you on a routine basis. If you have to find a new route to work so you don't drive by your former favorite coffee house, then so be it. Or, if you have to avoid the movie theater because you are afraid you won't enjoy your movie without popcorn, then just avoid it for now. (Or, do what my mom does... she puts "Vicks Vapor Rub" under her nose so when she walks by the concession stand, she's not tempted by the smell of the popcorn). It is only temporary as you get used to your lifestyle. This really helped accelerate my transition to Raw food because I didn't think about things that tempted me nearly as much. I was able to stay focused on Raw and its amazing health benefits. Feeling deprived was rarely an issue because I no longer focused on the things I was no longer eating. This tip alone can make all the difference.

SOCIAL SITUATIONS & PEER GROUPS

When it comes to the Raw lifestyle, one of the biggest hurdles for people has to do with social occasions. To this I say... *raise your standards*. This includes your peer group. Now, family is another issue. You will always have your family (whether they are supportive of what you are doing or not), but your peer group you can choose. Love your family and choose your peer group. Hence, pick wisely. This is one of the keys to setting yourself up to win. Very important! Your life is typically a reflection of your peer group's expectations. Whether it's family or friends, they might not be excited about what you are doing. The reason for this is because the changes you are making to better your health incidentally shine the light on *their* lifestyle choices. *Important:* This is not your fault, it's theirs. You might never say a word to them about their diet, but you will almost certainly encounter people who object to the idea of Raw (and vegan in general) because they feel that *their* way of life is under scrutiny.

It's a very strange and emotionally loaded issue for many people. If you told someone that you like, say, folk music, they wouldn't require that you defend your preference, or go on about how they must have their classic rock. However, if you told them that you only listened to classical music, then they might take offense because they assume—through no fault of yours—that you look down upon them. This is the key issue: People do crazy things to defend their egos. Many people will assume, from your dietary choices, that you think you are somehow superior to them... not just their food choices, but actually *them*. They will say the strangest things, and bring up the subject of food around you when it's not even relevant to the conversation. It's as though they're obsessing on the subject even when it's the furthest thing from your mind. (This is most common among people with the worst diets and those who have never met a vegan, which varies greatly depending on which part of the country you typically roam.) Depending on who they are, and how they behave, this obsessiveness can manifest as anything from genuine curiosity to rude and uninformed challenges to your chosen lifestyle. (Fear not; you will quickly evolve responses to handle any situation.)

Some of your peers do not want to admit—especially to themselves—that they might not be making the best choices. Not just for themselves, but for what they feed their families (and that's a whole other set of emotions... *am I being a good parent???*). But the real soul-searching is to be done by you: Do your peers have a low standard for their own health and well-being? Ask yourself that and think about the people with whom you spend most of your discretionary time. If you choose to spend time with people who don't share roughly similar health values, and if circumstances or personalities are such that this is always an issue, then they can quickly bring you down.

For most of my adult life, I have spent a fair share of my spare time in the gym, so many people in my peer group tend to strive for a healthy lifestyle. Even so... these people didn't necessarily support my going Raw. But I knew I was at least headed in the right direction with a good peer group, because they valued health. I knew they would be open to learning about my Raw experience if they could see it working for me. So, I did a "wait and see." It was great because it worked. I started experiencing major gains in my exercise routine, and they were able to witness it for themselves. I was no longer drinking all the yucky protein shakes while plugging my nose, and I wasn't taking over-the-counter stimulants either (like they were). The point here is that my peer group had similar health goals with respect to exercise and wanting a healthy body, but they didn't originally agree with the Raw (or even vegan) lifestyle to achieve those goals.

I also had some friends in my peer group who were not into healthy living much at all. I had a higher standard for my health than they did and it actually bothered them, although this is not something they would admit. They would try to get me to eat like they did because they were afraid to lose me, or because if I ate it, it would validate their lifestyle. This became a problem and I had to do some real soul searching about whether it was smart for me to hang around this kind of influence. Even if I didn't give in, there would always be a slight discord, a lack of harmony in that kind of setting. It might be small, but it's still negative, and not the kind of thing I want to submit myself to for very long.

My health is a priority because it makes everything else in my life better, so I take this very seriously. As a result, I had to rearrange and even change my peer group. When you create your peer group with people who are *doing better than you at the things you value for yourself*, they become an asset rather than a liability. You suddenly have to strive and work harder to keep up with them.

To improve my "health game" even more, I look to the experts. I buy books, audio CDs, DVDs, and anything I can get my hands on so that I'm constantly surrounded by it. I read and re-read their books because they continue to teach me and inspire me to be the best I can be. Another great option is to hire a Raw Lifestyle coach and there are plenty available. These people can help you reach your goals faster than you would on your own, because, with a coach, you're accountable. It's amazing what we'll do to live up to somebody else's expectations of us even when we don't always feel like living up to our own self-expectations.

I still continue my education by attending other classes and reading whatever I can get my hands on. It does not stop with classes, community meet-ups, books, DVDs and audio CDs; I also attend events with like-minded people such as potlucks, seminars, expos, etc. There are lots of events around the world for Raw food, and you should attend them whenever you can. There are also plenty of retreats and resorts that specialize in Raw food, detoxing, cleansing, relaxing, etc. Consider spending your next vacation at one of those places.

Throw a Fun Raw Food Party

Your social life does not have to end simply because you now eat the healthiest cuisine in the world. Have a fun Raw food prep party. One of the reasons people are intimidated by Raw food (this includes your family and friends) is because they know nothing about it, such as how to make it, what to eat, and most importantly, "why." By now, *you* might know it's really simple, but your family and friends might not. One of the best ways to get them involved is to have a party where you teach them how to make Raw food. I find it hard to believe that anyone would turn down an afternoon or evening of eating the healthiest food in the world (maybe alongside a glass of organic vegan wine). This is a fantastic way to help others learn about Raw food. Promise your friends a lot of fun and delicious food to eat. When I host my Raw food prep parties, I pick out 4-5 recipes that my friends and I will prepare. Before the party, I make copies of the recipes and buy all of the ingredients. I tell my friends to bring some containers to take leftovers home. I serve wine, put on some fun music, and I have all of my favorite Raw food books out for browsing. We have a blast!

Most of all, it gives people a chance to actually *taste* the food! Sounds obvious, but people really have no idea what the heck you're talking about until they try some of these delicious recipes. That's when the light bulb goes on. Prior to that, they assume you mean veggie platters and boring old salads.

Be Prepared When People Offer You Food

Part of succeeding with Raw socially is having standard responses ready when people offer you food. Naturally, you can always say, "thank you, but I'm vegan," but this often invites a conversation that you might not want to have at that moment. If you're not in the mood to go there, here are some good replies to have ready:

- I just ate a little while ago. (If you're like me, it's rare that you haven't eaten something—like a piece of fruit—fairly recently.)

- Thank you, but I'm on a strict regimen of Raw fruits and vegetables. Doctor's orders. ☺

- I'm addicted to sugar (or salt) and I won't be able to have just one unfortunately, so I have to pass, but thank you.

- I brought something for myself so I'm all set, thank you. (This is a great opportunity to offer them a taste of what you brought.)

Another great method is to ask people to help you achieve your goal, and in the future to not offer you these things. Most people—at least, the ones worth hanging out with— *will want to help you if you ask them for help.* If they can be a part of it, they usually jump at the chance. Tell them you've never been happier or felt better and you don't want to ruin it. This can be very effective for people in your peer group who don't share the same health goals. If they're able to support you and help you, even if they don't do it for themselves, then this can be a great way to stay in the same groups without constantly having to defend yourself.

The fundamental point here is that it's too easy to give in to cravings or peer pressure if you are not prepared. If you have some ready-made responses for when people offer you something, you are setting yourself up to win. You will find that this is needed less and less over time because you get stronger as time goes by and the people in your life get the point.

CHAPTER 10

MORE SURE-FIRE WAYS TO SUCCEED

Here are some more proven ways to succeed and stay on the road to high health by living the Raw lifestyle with ease.

EAT *LOTS* OF RAW FOOD

Eat as much Raw food as you need so you do not feel hungry or deprived, especially in the beginning when you are new to this lifestyle. Make yourself a deal that if you're craving something that is not on your plan - have something Raw instead. Maybe it's a treat that you love, whether it's a chocolate nut milk, green smoothie, pasta el pesto, or a Raw chocolate cookie. Eat until you don't want anymore and you're satiated. When you want a snack, have something that is Raw.

BE FOCUSED AND ORGANIZED

The more focused you are, the less overwhelming it is. One of the best things you can do for yourself with respect to Raw is to be organized. A great way to do this is to get a calendar dedicated as your "Raw Kitchen & Food Prep" calendar. Use this to schedule the food you want to eat 3-7 days in advance. Then, pick out some recipes that sound delicious to you, and make a shopping list. Next, write on the calendar any specific steps that need to be done ahead of time. For example, if you're going to have a pate-stuffed red bell pepper for lunch on Wednesday, then on Tuesday, you need to soak the nuts or seeds overnight so you can prepare the pate on Wednesday. You'll find that such planning becomes second nature after you've done it for about a month or two and you probably won't need the calendar as much, unless you're planning something special such as a holiday party, celebration, or maybe when you're making a dish that is new to you. The steps it takes to be organized take only minutes, which is nothing compared to the time and energy you will save.

BE PREPARED

Having food prepared is one of the easiest sure-fire ways to succeed living the Raw lifestyle. When you are hungry or you want a snack, it's as simple as walking to your refrigerator and eating some great Raw food. Keep bowls of fresh fruit and Raw trail mix on your counter and within reach. Just seeing the delicious food is motivating and reminds you of your healthy lifestyle.

For the times when you are not home, it is critical to be prepared. Have snacks and food with you at all times. This applies to both short as well as long outings. I have a little bag that I take with me to restaurants which has a tiny bottle of Raw olive oil, my Himalayan salt in a little jar, cayenne pepper, and a few other small things. I get lemon wedges from the restaurant and then I can always dress up a salad or plain veggies.

Buy yourself a special cooler to use in your car (mine is a medium-sized, soft-sided cooler), fill it with ice packs, and put food in it for the day when you go to work, events, family gatherings, anything. If I'm away from home for even half a day, I pack my cooler with fruit, veggies, seeds/nuts, ice, salad, green smoothie, etc. I can head out for the day without worrying at all that I'll be stuck somewhere and get hungry. You never know when it may happen; you might find yourself in a traffic jam or an unexpectedly long appointment. This preparation makes all the difference in the world. Trust me, it makes your life much easier.

I sometimes call ahead to restaurants, and usually the chef is more than pleased to accommodate my special request for vegan food or a nice Raw vegetable and fruit plate. I also have a small laminated card I carry in my wallet that I give to the waiter to show the chef. It reads: "Hello, I eat raw plant-based foods. I'd greatly appreciate it if you could make me a plate with any of the following on it"... then I list a bunch of different fruits, veggies, olives, etc. It's a great way to give the chef ideas of things you eat. And, if you like what the chef prepared, make sure the chef and manager know how pleased you were.

If it's a family or business outing, I try to let people know what to expect of me beforehand. This helps eliminate any awkwardness if I bring my own dish to a function, meeting or social time. It's a great conversation starter too, because people always ask me "why." Moreover, I tend to bring a little "extra" for others to sample, if they seem interested. This is a great way to spread the word about Raw. A note of caution here though, some restaurants won't let you bring in outside food, so if you bring something of your own, do it inconspicuously.

If I find myself in a situation where I don't see something on the menu, or I didn't bring my own food to someone's house, I like to use it as an excuse to relax my digestive system and just drink water or herbal tea. It is not always easy, but it gets easier every time. It becomes empowering—having the knowledge that you have total control over what goes into your body. I'm always aware that I am only a couple hours away (at the most) from my delicious and healthy Raw, organic vegan food.

Here is another tip, although obvious to most, is that you can also make sure you eat something before you go, such as any of the following:

- Two bananas

- An apple or two

- A tablespoon of nut or seed butter

- Three dates

- A fresh green smoothie or green juice

Some ideas to order at restaurants: At Mexican restaurants I typically eat guacamole and salsa and I might bring my own flax chips or strips of fresh red bell pepper to dip into them. (Tortilla chips are often vegan, but not always. And not only are they cooked, but they are deep fried, which is very unhealthy due to the presence of trans-fats, which are as bad as cholesterol.)

At other kinds of restaurants, I typically get a salad (or even two), or if they have a vegetable side dish, I'll ask to have it Raw and order a couple of them. I squeeze lemon on it, drizzle some olive oil and sprinkle some of the salt that I carry with me and voila... it's fantastic.

For longer trips, I do the same, but I take more things such as seeds, ready-made dehydrated foods, and all sorts of other stuff. It just depends on the trip. For much more about traveling Raw, see chapter 15.

CREATE A LIST OF ACTIVITIES... NOW!

I wish I could say, "Oh, it's easy and you should naturally just want to eat Raw all the time, and once you start, you'll never look back or desire cooked food again." However, very few people adopt the lifestyle by going 100% cold turkey (so to speak) and stick with it forever. It's much more likely that there will be some speed bumps in the road. We live in a society where we are bombarded with ads for addictive unhealthy foods and we are surrounded by many places and people that, not only do not support optimal health, it's not even in their best interest to do so.

Maybe if I had been eating Raw food since I was born, it would be much easier to deal with, but I wasn't. Or, maybe if I lived in a beautiful log cabin in the woods, where I grew my own food, or if I lived two minutes away from a farmer's market, it might be easier to stay Raw. But, I don't. And, you probably don't either. In order to thrive and succeed *with great ease and happiness* about your Raw lifestyle (and that's part of the key... being excited and happy), I find that it helps my clients, and myself, to be prepared, organized, and to do things like I am suggesting in this book. I love the Raw lifestyle and I love the way it makes me feel, but I have made it easy on myself by doing the things I have written about here.

Create a list of activities. This list is going to be important for you, especially during any challenges you might encounter. A typical challenge is avoiding temptation and addictive cooked food *at night*. Remember that you'll feel the best about yourself to the degree that you feel you are in control of your every day choices and in control of your life. The more control you have over the choices you make, the more empowered you feel and the less stress you experience. There are things you can't always control such as traffic, weather, and other people, but you can control what you eat. And, when you eat a Raw healthy diet, it makes dealing with those other issues out of your control much easier to deal with.

Make a List

To start, make a list of things you have always wanted to do, learn, or try, and if one of those "hard" times is upon you, then go research something on your list or go do one of them. Get specific and make a file for each one so that you can easily store information or ideas as you research certain activities. This is where you'll accumulate things that support the items on your list.

Making this list is rewarding for two reasons. First, you now have a list of things to do, to distract you from eating cooked addictive food. Second, you get excited because you are actually setting goals and ideas for your life that you can look forward to.

Some of the items on the list will require research on the Internet and that activity alone is something that distracts you from thinking about food—and the more excited about the thing, the better. The other items on the list are things or hobbies that you actually want to take up right away, such as yoga, dancing lessons, etc. By filling your life with fun and different activities, you become more fulfilled and—very importantly—thinking much less about diet and food. In fact, when you do think about food, it will be in this new context, and you will be more and more excited about your new dietary choices, and thinking less and less about your old habits.

Divide your list into two sections: 1) Things that you have not yet done that you want to do before you die, and 2) things you have done and enjoy.

On my list of things to do, I have things like… learn Italian, visit family in Italy (travel Europe in general) and Australia, go on a Safari to see beautiful wild animals, venture to China (list the cities and activities you want to do on your trips), learn yoga, learn about World War II, run a marathon, learn about photography, read the books on philosophy that I've collected, start my holiday shopping list, get two new Raw recipes from the Web, etc. The list is endless and I'm always adding to it. The important thing is that you give yourself tons and tons of options for activities to do so you are *not thinking about food*. Keep this list handy. Keep a copy of this list posted on your refrigerator so the next time you mindlessly wander into your kitchen for food because you have nothing better to do… well, now you'll see that *you have something better to do!*

Next, make your list of things that aren't new to you (that you know you'd enjoy), but that will give you something to do in those moments when you feel like giving in to a craving for something that isn't healthy. For me, this can be accomplished by reading a great book, listening to some jamming music that makes me want to be fit and get up and dance, calling my brother to chat, vacuuming and washing the floors, doing some jumping jacks, taking a 10-minute walk. Whatever it is, even if it's all of the above... promise yourself to do something related to one of these *before* eating the food. If you are not *truly* hungry (many cravings are just from boredom, habit, positive associations, smells, etc.), you're probably thinking about food because of emotional eating or mindlessly because you're bored or because you crave something unhealthy as a result of an addiction that is not cleaned out of your system yet. After doing one or all of those "other" activities from your list, if you still need or want the food, then have half the amount and call it a day.

You see, even doing this, you're still a success because you didn't do as badly as you would have done otherwise. That's remarkable—*be proud!* The next time it happens, you will do even better. It really does become easier.

AVOID TEMPTATION

I mean this. Really... it works. Remember the saying:

Out of sight, out of mind.

Stay away from temptation, at least in the beginning. Literally remove the tempting thing from your sight, your sense of smell, your travel pattern, your pantry, etc. During periods of non-craving, throw stuff away. If you're addicted to popcorn in the movies, then don't go to the movies until you think you can handle going without indulging. If driving by a certain coffee shop on your way to work has a way of magically steering your car into the shop's parking lot, then take an alternate route to work. If going out with friends for happy hour means having a glass of wine, which will weaken your resolve and cause you to eat unhealthy cooked food, then skip happy hour and call your friends later instead. Or just order an orange juice. If you want to get a little fancy, order an orange juice with club soda and a twist of lime. It's delicious.

JUST MOVE

Moving the body changes the brain's mental state. Any time you are experiencing a craving or doubts, don't think big picture (long-term benefits are not as real to the brain as short-term benefits, or short-term discomfort). Instead, think about the five minutes *immediately in front of you and.. get your body moving!*

- Stand up and stretch

- Breathe deeply

- Take a walk around the block or even just up and down your street (this one is easy and can be done virtually anywhere, so—no excuses!)

- Walk up and down a few flights of stairs if you're in a multi-story building

- Do jumping jacks, wherever you are

- Jump rope (this too can be done almost anywhere)

- Go swimming

- Do yoga

- Do push-ups

- Go the gym

- Go to the mall and just walk, walk, walk

- Go to a park (or the beach, if you happen to live near one)

TAKE A BREAK FROM FOOD PREP

You may not always feel like fixing your own food, yet there aren't many great Raw choices at restaurants. That's okay, with a little bit of planning... there are a few places that ship Raw meals nationally! Treat yourself to this once in a while. This will give you a few days worth of food and you won't have to think about preparing it... just enjoy. The two I know of (and there may be more) are RAWvolution.com and PureRawCafe.com.

GET A PET

Even if it is a goldfish or turtle... but the best is to adopt a pet in need of a home. Pets are great for helping you place your attention someplace other than yourself and food. Studies have shown that just having a pet nearby makes us more calm.

GO RAW WITH A BUDDY OR LOVED ONE

An easy way to succeed living the Raw lifestyle is to do this with a buddy or loved one. It's fun and exciting. You can test recipes together, exercise together, and share ideas and information. You can buy in bulk, thereby getting a better discount on the food, and split it up. You can prepare Raw food dishes and have a food exchange, where you make a big batch of a particular recipe, and give half to your buddy and vice versa. This helps save time and money, and adds variety without adding work.

REWARDS IN THE MAIL

This is one of my favorites! Ordering things. It's really fun and exciting to order new things for your new Raw lifestyle. Do a little shopping every few weeks, even if it is to buy a new flavor of flax crackers, a cool organic cotton t-shirt, a new book, a tool for your kitchen, a box of Raw food from a place that ships nationally, or some organic hand cream. Don't buy things you don't need or won't use, and you don't need to spend a lot of money. And don't buy them all at once... the idea here is the "drip" or "trickle" theory where you send yourself something every few weeks, like a little drip. This is exciting to do, gives you something to look forward to, acts as a constant reminder of what you are doing, and it *refreshes your momentum*.

GET EDUCATED AND INSPIRED FOR RAW

Surround yourself with this amazing lifestyle. *Immerse yourself*. Start learning more and more about it every chance you get, taking full advantage of everything you can get your hands on. Here are a couple of ways you can do that.

- *Read!* I get inspired when I flip through a book about Raw food, even if I have already read it (many times!). Simply reminding myself of how others have succeeded with Raw is very powerful. I'm drawn to testimonials of people succeeding with Raw so I read these frequently. Most Raw books have testimonials and they are abundant on the Internet. Another place to look for inspiration is recipe books. I hear this all the time from people who purchase my recipe books, but it works for me too!... I'm *constantly* reading my own recipe books to plan and get excited about what I'll be making the following week and how great I'll feel from eating all of the fresh organic food. It becomes very habit-forming!

- **Watch videos and listen to audios!** Here are some DVDs that I highly recommended. They don't cover a Raw diet, rather, one covers eating a plant-based diet and the other discusses genetically modified foods (which if you don't know about, or thought it was just politics or hand-wringing by alarmists, I'm here to tell you that you should learn more because the facts are very disturbing and will outrage you.) These DVDs contain a great deal of information. I watch these repeatedly. Sometimes I just have it playing in the background while I'm getting ready in the morning to get my mind set for the day. Yes, I still do this!

- Recommended DVDs:

  - *Eating*
    available at ravediet.com/ordernu.html
  - *The Future of Food*
    available at Amazon.com
  - *Earthlings*
    available at PETA.org

After you have watched these a few times, you may also like to pass them along to somebody else, or better yet, donate them to your library, to help get the word out. I keep mine because I like to watch them from time to time, but I lend them out to people all the time... this is democracy in action, true grass roots—the way that fringe ideas start to become mainstream. Tip: Be sure to write your name on the case with a Sharpie to make sure you get it back! Or if you give it to someone, make them promise to pass it along to someone else.

- **Take classes!** You need to immerse yourself and make your new lifestyle second nature to you. This will accelerate your transition and keep you energized and excited well after the newness has worn off. Sign up for local Raw food prep classes and seminars. Even if you're learning basic things you think you already know, you can always learn something new from different teachers. Students tell me all the time that they love coming to all of my classes because they find them to be inspiring and motivating. Sometimes you even learn from others attending the class. The gathering of students and like-minded individuals with the same goal is powerful. Don't underestimate this powerful component. If classes are not offered in your area, then start asking for them. Go to local health food stores, community ed classes at your local community college and leave word that you're interested in classes on "Raw Food Preparation." *(Then have your friends call and do the same!)*

- **Get online!** Check out Raw web sites, join online forums where you can answer other people's questions or get answers to some of your own questions. Watch YouTube videos of people preparing Raw food or talking about how they are succeeding with the Raw food lifestyle. Read Raw Vegan blogs where they discuss living the lifestyle. There are many! This is especially important if you are doing this without the support of your family or friends, because you will see all of these other people around the world and you'll realize that you are not alone.

- **Community!** Another way to surround yourself with like-minded people is in your community through get-togethers, activities, potlucks, etc. Check out Meetup.com, where there are plenty of different Raw, health, and fitness-oriented groups in your local area and join them. Don't look for Raw exclusively, mix it up with people who are vegetarians, vegans, and into alternative health. These are the groups that are particularly open-minded to Raw. And, don't be afraid to attend these meetings all by yourself; in fact, most people usually do. If you can't find a group near you, then start one yourself and use meetup.com to advertise it.

- **Start sprouting!** (See directions at the end of this book.) Sprouting is a great and inexpensive tool that serves as a reminder of who you are now. Growing your own sprouts is so amazing and rewarding as you watch these little babies grow before your eyes day by day! It's very cool. And, they're delicious and super nutritious. Add them to salads, smoothies, and soups, eat them plain, top your pate with them, take them in a Ziploc to go for your car, and more! Growing your own sprouts is one of the easiest, most satisfying (both the growing and the eating) and most exciting ways to inspire your Raw lifestyle.

- **Stop mindless eating!** There is a phenomenal book called, *Mindless Eating* by Brian Wansink, Ph.D., director of the Cornell University Food and Brand Lab in Ithaca, New York. He has been studying the field of food psychology for over 20 years. He has discovered some amazing and ground-breaking findings related to people's eating habits. I highly recommend the book. Here are some of Dr. Wansink's interesting findings that could help:

"There are five major areas where people tend to overindulge: dinnertime, snacking, at restaurants, at parties, and desktop/dashboard dining. The music, the number of dinner companions, how long we're sitting at one table—all of these factors affect how much we'll eat."

Solution: Take advantage of this by being more mindful when you're eating and not mindless. Part of the key to succeeding here is to be prepared. Know ahead of time that you might need to leave a party early or get up from the dinner table after a short period of time instead of lingering there.

Solution: When snacking, use smaller portions and do not snack from the whole jar. Take out a small portion, put it on a plate and enjoy. When eating while at your desk or in the car, again, portion control will definitely help prevent overeating. Always serve yourself less than you think you might want. Just remember, the food is not going anywhere, so if you are still hungry after eating the smaller portion, then you can always get more (but there's a good chance you won't). But if you take more at the beginning, you're almost certain to eat it just because it's there. Again, Dr. Wansink:

"Our eye judges amounts by using contextual cues, so a helping of mashed potatoes on a 12-inch plate, for example, is going to look like less than it would on an 8-inch plate. If you think you're too smart to be fooled, think again."

Solution: Take advantage of this by using mini-size bowls and plates. Replace short, wide glasses with tall, skinny ones. A tall glass that holds the same amount of liquid as a short glass seems like there is more because our brains register height rather than width.

REST

Getting adequate rest is a critical component to well-being and optimal health. I am not just referring to sleep either. I am referring to making it a point, every day if possible, to take 5-15 minutes and just rest. Rest your eyes. Quiet your mind. Think about the sky, or the sun, or the trees. Something that is calming. Or, think about nothing at all, if you're capable of this (if you're not, it's a very important skill to learn, and it's not very hard if you take a quick, 1-session introductory meditation class). Take an occasional warm bath; light a candle, soak in some aromatherapy bath salts or oils and just relax. Don't use the time to reflect on the day you just completed or for planning the following day, for that matter. Just take the 15 minutes to think about the blue sky, the color of clouds, the fall leaves as they change colors, the ocean and the beach, a bird flying... even the pattern of plaster on the wall—it doesn't matter what; just let it happen. Your life will change remarkably by incorporating this 5-15 minutes into each day.

Power naps are another fantastic way to get rest and increase your energy, if your routine allows it. Cornell psychologist Dr. James Maas, author of *Power Sleep*, says a twenty-minute nap in the afternoon actually provides more rest than sleeping an extra twenty minutes in the morning. Be sure not to nap longer than thirty minutes however, or you can find it difficult to wake up!

"True silence is the rest of the mind, and it is to the spirit what sleep is to the body— nourishment and refreshment."

— William Penn

GRATEFULNESS AS A PART OF YOUR EVERY DAY

When you are grateful, you are rich. I learned a long time ago that one of the best remedies when feeling down or stressed is to think about three things for which you are grateful. Your mindset changes *immediately*. I bring this important topic up because, when you are grateful, you become addicted to taking care of yourself because you realize how much you have and what you could lose.

It's a regular practice for me *everyday* to think about the reasons I am grateful. Here are some of the things that I think: "I'm so grateful that I have vision to see and read books, which I love to do. I'm grateful for my dog. I'm grateful for my car and for the food in my refrigerator (there are people without these things, you know)." If you still need convincing, I urge you to volunteer for a homeless shelter, or take an eye-opening trip to a developing country. There is no quicker way to become grateful than to see what others don't have. And if you want to know the value of health, just ask anybody who doesn't have it.

It's so simple to begin. All you have to do is start each day when you wake up thinking about three things that you're grateful you have in your life.

NEVER GIVE UP...

"Never give up. This may be your moment for a miracle."

— Greg Anderson

If you fall off the wagon, don't be discouraged! Sometimes the harder you fall, the stronger the momentum you have to get back up. You'll find yourself equipped with an even stronger mindset that nothing will stop you. Use this to your advantage. Be encouraged. I like what Tony Robbins (the personal growth expert) has to say, "When you're frustrated, that is the time to get excited—*because you are about to have a breakthrough.*"

I've been there; I know how it can be. There have been times that I fell off the Raw lifestyle for part of the day, and since cooked food can have addictive qualities, I would end up finishing the day with even more cooked food. Then, even though I promised myself that on the following day I would clean it up, I would still have something cooked. Finally, I would get fed up with mistreating my body, noticing unhealthy and uncomfortable physical changes after only a couple of days or less of being "off" and it motivated me to take back control.

Looking back at the times I went off course... each time, they became shorter in duration and less severe because I was making better choices over time. The story is not how many times you fall; rather, if you fall off, how long do you stay off? How quickly can you get back on and learn from it? And, learn you will! You learn more about yourself every time. You make progress, you grow, and you become more proud of your accomplishments every day. You become stronger every time you do something new or learn new things about yourself and it empowers you. Don't be discouraged if you slip. Just get right back on, starting with your *next meal*. It's that simple. You will get stronger every time because each time you'll learn more about yourself. You'll know from previous experience how quickly you can rally, meaning you won't be afraid and get demoralized. You'll also start to gather more Raw vs. Not Raw data points and realize that you consistently feel the best when you eat Raw, and this will help keep you on track in the future.

Any time I went off my Raw path, I always got right back on. It might have taken a day or two of reflection to rebound, but I did it. It was during these reflections I recognized that each time I was actually a little better to myself. One of the first times I went off the Raw path I had a vegan burrito, soy cappuccino and vegan cookies (okay, maybe it was THREE cookies)—all in one meal. I'm telling you this because even I—*a Raw Food Chef!*—have gone off the path, and more than once. But I learned from it and jumped right back on. The first time I went off, it lasted a couple weeks. The next time, it lasted about one week, the next was just a few days, and so on. And, each time, I made better choices despite the hiccup. I went from three cookies, to two cookies, to one cookie. I can't emphasize enough the importance of acknowledging your incremental victories; these are part of the normal process and a type of success.

I promise—it gets easier. There can be times that you fall off but you get stronger each time you get back on. Eventually, you naturally gravitate back toward Raw or High Raw, because at some deep level, your mind and body know that's where you belong.

> *"Tomorrow is the most important thing in life.*
> *Comes into us at midnight very clean.*
> *It's perfect when it arrives and it puts itself in*
> *our hands. It hopes we've learned something*
> *from yesterday."*
>
> — John Wayne

CHAPTER 11

GET FAMILY SUPPORT

SEEK THE SUPPORT OF YOUR FAMILY AND KIDS

One of the first questions people ask about going Raw is how to get family support. Remember the importance of the example you are setting for your family. It might not always be easy, but it's worth it because you are leading by example (and if it's your kids, it's your responsibility to provide them with the healthiest habits you can, or at least with the best information available, if they're older). Here are some tips and tricks that I've seen work wonders on even the most stubborn families:

1. Start slowly when you are introducing this to your family. In fact, it should probably be a slow transition for you, too. Go slow, whether it's just you that's transitioning, or their diet too.

2. Involve your family and ask for their support, whether it's just for you or for the whole family. When you ask your family to support you, it makes them a part of your process and experience. In life, I think it's fundamental that people *want* to help. And, when they are asked to support you, it can completely change their mindset and view of what you are doing. Suddenly the focus is on you and not on them. I think that people naturally start looking at their own behaviors when someone else is making changes. This can cause problems because

sometimes people do not want to admit they are doing anything wrong. So, if you ask them to help you, they don't even realize it, but the focus is off of them and they are in a better mindset to support you. Eventually, as they see such phenomenal health changes in you, they actually want to try it themselves, with no defensiveness because you never confronted their lifestyle. This is one of the best ways for family to get on board—doing so voluntarily—because it usually means a much higher success rate.

3. Get your family's opinion and take requests for recipes. Show your family different Raw recipes from books and the Internet, and let them take turns picking out which recipes you make for them to try. Or, ask your family for some of their favorite flavors and pick out something to make based on that. This is especially helpful for kids because it makes them think they're making a choice, which gives them some ownership in the process.

4. Okay, if you know your family won't go for the support and ownership stuff, forget all that... *be stealthy!* Start making one Raw dish at every dinner or every other dinner, and don't even mention it. Again, start slowly and incorporate more over time—they probably won't even realize they are eating so much Raw food, except that they will start feeling so great! I recommend starting with a side dish that is Raw, or a soup that is Raw. (*Warm the soup in your dehydrator briefly if that makes it more appealing to your family. Or, you can warm it on the stove, lowest setting, using your finger to stir it. By using your finger and being able to do that without it hurting, means it's at a temperature that maintains the integrity of the nutrients and enzymes.*)

Another idea is to start introducing your family to Raw by making a Raw dessert. When kids and family start getting to eat dessert after every meal, that is especially exciting, especially when they can have second helpings of it. In no time at all, you'll be having a Raw side dish and a Raw dessert with every meal.

5. Bigger salads. This goes in line with #4 above. Start preparing big beautiful salads with vibrant colors and fresh Raw salad dressings. A great way to present these is using big plates (as opposed to bowls where things can fall to the bottom). This way, you can see all of the beautiful fresh produce at once. The best salads, especially for people new to Raw, include things like red bell peppers, olives, raisins, tomatoes, cucumbers, great lettuce, and delicious Raw dressing (see my book *Kristen Suzanne's EASY Raw Salads & Dressings*). One of the tricks is keeping the salads simple, but varied every day. So, one night, you might make a salad with red bell peppers, tomatoes, raisins and olives. Then, the next night you might make a salad with orange bell peppers, cucumbers, olives, blueberries or blackberries. Then, the next night, make a similar salad but change the lettuce and add chopped pecans or walnuts. Change the dressing every couple of days, too. All of this makes it a very exciting, well-balanced and delicious experience for your whole family. You can also cut the veggies and fruit in different shapes with inexpensive kitchen tools to add variety. Kids notice this, too!

6. Serve in *courses*—by filling up with delicious, huge salads, you and your family will eat much less cooked food. One way to ensure you succeed with this plan is to only have the food you're eating on the table at a given

sitting. For example, while you're eating the huge salads, just have the salads on the table. Don't distract your family with having bread or crackers or even the main entrée at the table while you are eating the salad. This way they concentrate on the salad, taking their time, enjoying all of it and not focusing on anything else. And if they're very hungry, they'll wolf down a lot of it. Then, when you are done with the salads, bring out the entrée. Do the same process and follow with dessert.

7. Start making certain meals Raw. The easiest way to do this is to start making breakfast 100% Raw. You can start by drinking fresh organic smoothies for breakfast, eating plenty of fresh fruit, or having fresh cinnamon nut milk with Raw granola. Again, it will greatly help if you let your family take part in choosing what flavors to make. So, the night before you make a smoothie, ask your kids (and/or your significant other, etc.) which flavors they would like to create. Make it fun by talking about the different colors, too. I love getting my nephews excited about drinking Green Smoothies. I give it a much cooler name, however: "Dragon Smoothies," or "Incredible Hulk Smoothies"... *they love that!* Or, make a strawberry and banana smoothie and call it "Barbie's Smoothie." Trust me... these things help! Other breakfast suggestions would be Raw granola with a deliciously, sweet nut or seed milk (Raw vegan milk recipes are available in my book, *Kristen Suzanne's EASY Raw Vegan Smoothies, Juices, Elixirs and Drinks*). Let's not forget the spectrum I wrote about earlier though. Let's say your family typically eats conventional cereal with dairy milk. Then let them eat the cereal but have them try fresh organic Raw nut milk with it instead. This is a huge step. Ask them which kind

of nut milk they'd like (almond, pecan, sesame seed, walnut, macadamia, hemp—*my favorite*, etc.) Find out if they'd like Raw Chocolate in the nut milk (YUM!) or maybe some cinnamon and nutmeg. Variety is a key component to success, as well as involving your family in the choice.

8. If anybody in your household is in a sport, urge them to try Raw to give them an edge in their game. This is particularly effective with teens.

9. Here is one of the best ideas (I love this): For every gift you are due to receive (Mother's Day, Father's Day, birthday, holiday, anniversary, etc.) ask that someone's (or your entire family's) gift to you be the gift of him/her/them going Raw (or even just Vegan) for a set period of time, such as a week or perhaps even a month). Let them know how much this gift would mean to you and thank them every day they're doing it as the best gift ever.

10. Do you need to get your little kids excited to eat more raw fruits and vegetables? Easy, try this great tactic: It's important to give your kids choices so they do not feel forced to eat just one thing. You can do this by offering them something really tasty compared to something that might not be as tasty, thereby making the tasty option seem that much better. For example, offer your kids a choice between blueberries and celery. They will probably pick the blueberries and be happy about it because they had a say in the matter and blueberries taste good (imagine how different this is than offering them blueberries or Oreos!) Or, make it a choice between carrots and zucchini. They'll probably pick the

carrots and be happy about it because of the alternative. This is an effective way to get more fruits and vegetables in your children's diets. Another super tip is to cut your children's fruit and veggies into fun shapes and sizes using inexpensive kitchen tools. (There are entire books about how to make fancy shapes with your produce.) Just imagine how much fun you can have doing this together.

11. Include your children in the experience of shopping and preparing the food. This really makes them feel more connected to the food and it makes them feel proud to have helped. When you're proud of something, you tend to want to partake more in it, and children experience the same thing. Let them help you shop and prepare the food. Have fun while you're doing it and be sure to thank them for their help.

12. Here is a great way to get your young children excited about eating naturally colorful, organic foods that come from the earth. Tell them that they get to eat a "rainbow of colors" each day. Get a piece of construction paper for every color of the rainbow - red, orange, yellow, green, blue, and purple. Then, have your children cut out a big, fun shape for each color. On one side of each shape, write the word "DONE" and draw a smiley face. Stick them on the front of your refrigerator door with the word "DONE" side down. Each day, as your kids eat a fresh fruit or vegetable that is a color of the rainbow, flip over that color's shape so the word "DONE" is face up and you can see it. It's a great way to motivate your kids and get them excited about eating all the colors of the rainbow, because they get a challenge and a sense of accomplishment.

13. Another great way to get your kids eating more fruits and vegetables: as appetizers. Family (kids especially) are usually hungry while you're making dinner, so they ask for snacks. Use this to get more fresh fruit and vegetables into their diets. Always keep a plate of carrot sticks (or other veggies) and fruit available on your counter while you're preparing dinner. Your family will almost always polish off the fruit and vegetables before you're done preparing the meal.

14. Kid lunch ideas: Kids love fruit, so give them plenty. You can also make flax crackers to dip in Raw almond butter and sweet berry jam. Raw desserts are also great for kids because they can be eaten any time of the day and kids love that! Giving your child a piece of Raw strawberry pie for lunch is fun and healthy. They also love hummus and fresh raw veggies to dip into it. You can also make many other delicious and nutritious dips for kids that are Raw and dairy-free. Best of all, kids love green smoothies because of the cool color. It's such an effective way to get more greens into their diets. You can use a little of the greens (small handful) at first with plenty of fruit, while they get used to it, which is always fast because they taste really great. Let them put the ingredients in the blender and push the button. This makes it fun for them! Then, get a neat thermos to put it in and send them off to school.

15. Play with your food: Make eating Raw food fun. You already have a head start because of the beautiful bright colors found in fresh fruit and vegetables. Now, take it to the next level...make stuff with the food. For example, make a smiley face out of a salad by using:

- Hair: Spring lettuce mix, spinach or spiralized zucchini

- Eyes: Grapes, blueberries, olives, or grape tomatoes

- Lips: Red bell pepper lips

- Ears: Zucchini or cucumber

- Nose: Carrot

Be sure to have some delicious Raw veggie dip in a little cup to the side.

Or make a playground:

- Swing set: Asparagus or julienne carrots

- Grass: Spinach chopped

- Merry-go-round: Thick tomato slice

- Trees/bushes: Broccoli

CHAPTER 12

A DAY IN THE LIFE OF RAW

What does someone's daily lifestyle look like when they are eating Raw cuisine and living the Raw lifestyle? While this varies for everyone, depending on individual goals, there are some common elements. One of the things I love about this lifestyle is that it can be applied to anyone, a little or a lot, at any stage of their life, and you can start to feel better immediately. Another exciting aspect is all the amazing food choices. It will never get boring or mundane. This is a lifestyle that people, all around the world, have adopted and stayed on for decades because they experience true health like never before. People love living the Raw lifestyle because it works. It's balanced. It's delicious. It's fun. It's easy. And, it's simply the healthiest lifestyle there is. This is why there are people who have been eating High Raw and 100% Raw diets for 20, 30, and 40 years. Once you do it, you always want to do it. You will feel better than you ever have emotionally, physically, mentally and spiritually.

Raw food can work for you whether you are short on time or whether you have multiple hours a week to prepare food. I'm able to easily make it work for me no matter what is going on in my life. When I'm pressed for time, I grab fresh, crisp apples or bananas for breakfast. When I have more time for food preparation, I make crunchy and sweet Raw granola with fresh hemp nut milk and strawberries. The wonderful thing about eating a Raw food diet is that it can be simple, easy, varied and still full of flavor.

BREAKFAST

Here are some examples of what I do for an energizing Raw breakfast. When I'm short on time, I simply eat fresh, delicious, sweet fruit. For example, I'll eat two, three or even four bananas. I'm also a huge fan of smoothies and green juice (I like to call it *Plant Blood*). My morning smoothies are usually made of a 2-3 pieces of fruit and a little water. I also love green smoothies... water, a couple pieces of fruit and a handful of greens. Delicious and fast. Another great thing about smoothies is that you can make a giant batch of them at once, then drink them over the next 2-3 days. They have a reasonably good shelf life if you store them in airtight containers in the refrigerator. Glass is healthier than plastic. I prefer glass mason jars, almost filled to the top with your smoothie so there is as little air in there as possible (to help prevent your smoothie from oxidizing).

Then, for days that I have a little more time, I will eat Raw granola with freshly made nut milk. That being said, granola is typically made before hand since you need to dehydrate it. Raw nut and seed milk can be made easily and quickly, on the spot, or you can make a large batch at the beginning of the week, for example, and then have it to drink for the week.

And finally, sometimes, I even eat a Raw dessert for breakfast. Why not? It's healthy!

LUNCH

Lunch has many delicious options available. Sometimes I eat a giant vegetable salad with a fantastic Raw dressing. Other times I drink a big green fruit smoothie so I'm getting nourishing minerals from the greens while receiving energy and vitamins from the fruit. Other times, I drink a satiating Raw soup alongside some flax crackers and Raw cheese spread. Soups and smoothies are fantastic for your digestive system and they can give you skyrocketing energy. They are also a great way to eat more greens, so you are getting filled with healthy body- and bone-building minerals. When I make a soup for my lunch, I make a large batch that lasts 2-3 days. I might eat it for 2-3 days in a row, but it's so delicious that I don't mind. For added variation with the soup, on the last day, I could use it as a sauce on zucchini pasta or I water it down (if needed) and use it as a dressing on a big salad of chopped vegetables. Food has never been so easy, simple, delicious and nutritious.

ENTREES

Dinner is a special time for eating because this is usually when we sit down with family. There are many options for entrees. From simple entrees such as pate stuffed in fresh red bell peppers, garden burgers or zucchini pasta marinara to more gourmet options like pizza, lasagna, or quiche... you'll find you and your family eating the most satiating, healthy and delicious food available in the world.

DESSERTS

Almost every dessert you'd normally cook, you can make Raw—in fact, it's usually easier! I don't know many people who do not like desserts. There might be people who don't eat them, but it's not usually because they don't like them (think: skinny super models). Well, I have excellent news for both you and them (the skinny models, that is). The greatest thing about Raw desserts is that they appeal to everyone. Raw desserts can be eaten any time of the day because they are healthy, especially as compared to a standard cooked dessert that's loaded with all kinds of processed sugar. Moreover, Raw desserts are much healthier than the normal breakfast foods that most people eat (scones, muffins, high sugar cereals drowning in milk, eggs and buttered toast—and don't even get me started on the heart-gunking insanity that is bacon and eggs!). It is not surprising to find me eating a Raw chocolate cookie... *for my breakfast*.

For things like mousse and pudding (which freeze well), I usually store them in 1-cup size mason jars. This way, I can take out a small jar for a couple of days while keeping the rest of it frozen, if I'm the only one eating it.

CHAPTER 13

GETTING STARTED

It's time to dive in and get started. In the following section, you are going to learn about food shopping, organic foods, stocking your kitchen, rules for selecting and ripening produce, food storage, setting up your Raw kitchen, soaking and dehydrating nuts and seeds, and time saving tips for the kitchen.

LET'S GO SHOPPING!

I would say the most important thing to remember when food shopping is to only buy what you need when it comes to perishables. When you buy too much, you tend to want to eat it "before it goes bad" to prevent wasting money even, if you are not hungry. That is a recipe for unwanted weight gain, so try and avoid it. I have learned to make the extra trip to the store each week, if necessary, so I don't buy as much in one venture. This way, I eat what I buy and nothing more.

Even though you may be making an extra trip to the store each week, the actual time spent in the store goes down, because the days of going up and down every aisle are over. You won't be buying much from the aisles in the middle of the store. The majority of your shopping will be done around the perimeter of the store, and mostly the produce section. I keep a big stock of various nuts and seeds on hand in my freezer so it's not something I have to buy when I go to the store. I buy most of the nuts and seeds online, in bulk, which saves time and money.

When you go food shopping, make a list based on the recipes you will be making over the next few days and use this as your guide. Do not spend a lot of time wandering around the store and getting tempted to buy foods you don't need, or that are less healthy than those on your menu plan. *Go in, buy your fresh produce, and get out.*

STOCKING YOUR KITCHEN WTH FOOD

Here are some basic foods that are good to have on hand. In my kitchen, you'll find the following things. Keep in mind, I feed primarily two people who eat High Raw. I make a lot of green juices, smoothies and salads, which account for a lot of the greens and fruit. I typically go the store twice a week (or once a week and have food delivered once a week) to make sure I have these things on hand, plus an extra trip if necessary for special ingredients. You might not need all of the following items all of the time, but it gives you an *idea* of what your refrigerator, counter and pantry could look like. There are some items (such as dates, tahini, etc.) that I don't buy every week because they last awhile and I don't use them as regularly... but I always keep them stocked. Important note: Unless it's unavailable, *all* items listed below will always be organic in my kitchen.

Refrigerator

1 head romaine lettuce (or 1 bag pre-washed lettuce)
1 bunch spinach (or 1 bag pre-washed)
1-2 bunches kale—usually *lacinato* because it's easier to wash and juice than *curly kale*
4-6 cucumbers
2 bunches celery
4 red or orange bell peppers
6 carrots
1 beet
5-6 zucchini
Fresh herbs (basil, dill, rosemary, and/or oregano, for example)
1/8 – 1/4 pound fresh ginger
1 head garlic

1-2 bunches parsley and/or cilantro
1 red or yellow onion
3-4 apples
4 lemons
1-4 oranges and/or limes (not always, but sometimes—depending on the menu for the week)
Seasonal fresh fruit (LOTS!)—this changes by season, but an example would be 1 pineapple, 2 mangos, 2-4 pints of various berries, 2 peaches, etc. This is in addition to any fruit already on this list)
Miso*
Raw tahini
Raw nut/seed butters
Raw apple cider vinegar
2 pounds dates
2 pounds raisins
1 pound dried cranberries
1 pound dried apples
1 pound dried pineapple
Tamari, wheat-free
Flax oil
Hemp oil
1/4 pound kalamata olives (or any of your choice)
Nutritional yeast
Organic vegan white wine
Probiotics Powder or Capsules

*Miso is a high-protein seasoning known for its role in Japanese cuisine. It's usually made from a combination of soybeans, cultured grain and sea salt by a fermentation process. Miso contains all of the essential amino acids, making it a complete protein. Miso is not Raw, but due to the presence of beneficial digestive enzymes, unpasteurized miso is considered to be a "living food."

Freezer

6 bananas (peeled and stored in Food Saver bags)
Nuts and seeds (LOTS!) – Many varieties
3-4 small bags frozen fruit (usually berries and cherries)
2 small bags frozen corn (or 6-10 ears of fresh corn that I bought in-season, shucked, and froze whole)
Dried, unsweetened coconut (usually about 6 cups)
Raw chocolate powder (usually about 1-2 pounds)

On the Counter

2-3 pounds bananas (in varying stages of the ripening process)
2-3 ripening avocados
3-6 tomatoes
Growing sprouts (alfalfa, mung, clover) in mason jars
Organic vegan red wine
1-2 watermelons (seasonal)

Pantry

Raw organic olive oil (from LivingTreeCommunity.com)
Wasabi powder
Extracts (vanilla, almond, cherry, peppermint, etc)—alcohol free if possible
Raw agave nectar
Rapadura (This is not Raw. It's organic, unrefined, and unbleached whole cane sugar.)
Sun-dried tomatoes
Sun-dried tomato powder (you have to make this yourself, but you can make a lot because it lasts a very long time)
Himalayan crystal salt
I have 30-35 assorted spices and herbs in my kitchen, but a handful of must-haves are:

- Cayenne
- Cinnamon
- Cumin
- Dill (dried)
- Garlic powder
- Ginger (ground)
- Italian seasoning
- Mexican seasoning and/or chili powder
- Nutmeg
- Onion powder

Seeds for sprouting
Coconut oil
Dried mushrooms
Raw carob powder
Assortment of herbal teas

142

A NOTE ABOUT HERBS

Hands down, fresh herbs taste the best and have the highest nutritional value. While I recommend fresh herbs whenever possible, you can substitute dried herbs if necessary. But only do so in a ratio of:

3 parts fresh to 1 part dried

Dried herbs impart a more concentrated flavor, which is why you need less of them. For instance, if your recipe calls for three tablespoons of fresh basil, you'll be fine if you use one tablespoon of dried basil instead.

CHANGING PRODUCE

There is an important concept to understand when preparing Raw food... fresh produce can vary in its composition of water, texture, sweetness, and even flavor, to some degree. There are times I have made marinara sauce and, to me, it was absolutely perfect in its level of sweetness. Then, the next time I made it, following the exact same quantities and directions, it tasted as though I added a smidge of sweetener. So produce absolutely does vary (only ever so slightly, so don't be alarmed). Aahhh, but here is the silver lining... this means you will never get bored living the Raw lifestyle because your recipes can change a little in flavor from time to time, even though you used the same recipe. Embrace this natural aspect of produce and love it for everything that it is.

This is much less of an issue with cooked food. Much of the flavor and most of the water is taken out of cooked food, so you typically get the same flavors and experience each and every time. Boring!

RIPENESS, STORAGE AND OTHER TIPS FOR FRESH PRODUCE

- I'll address freezing produce right away. When you freeze your own fresh fruit and veggies, you could lose up to 30% of the nutritional value. However, that's not so bad when you look at the bigger picture. It is much better than eating cooked food, which has lost the vast majority of its nutritional value. So, if you need to freeze some foods because you were able to buy them on sale and save money, then by all means... do it! This is the kind of thing that helps you succeed with Raw because it ensures you always have lots of ingredients on hand, making it easier for you to prepare dishes whenever you want. (Many people, myself included, opt to buy a separate freezer, space and money permitting—they cost about $600.) When you buy frozen *fruit*, the same principle applies in that you'll be getting less nutritional value, but you do still get most of it. The same does *not* apply for commercially frozen vegetables. When you buy commercially frozen vegetables, like corn and peas for example, you don't get much nutritional value, if any at all. Frozen vegetables are blanched prior to freezing which destroys most of the enzymes and nutrients. In short, they're cooked, not Raw.

- Bell peppers: Did you know that green bell peppers and red bell peppers are actually the same thing? The green ones have just not ripened yet. That's why the red ones always cost more; they have to wait longer before they can be harvested, in order to ripen properly. I say "properly" because you never want to eat fruit that is not ripe yet (bell peppers are a fruit, not a vegetable) I never use green bell peppers because they are not ripe. This is

144

why many people have a hard time digesting them (often belching after eating them). To truly experience the greatest health, it's important to eat fruits and vegetables at their peak ripeness. Therefore, make sure you only use red, orange, or yellow bell peppers—all of these are fully ripe. Store them in your refrigerator.

- Bananas: If you're like most people you probably think that a banana should be eaten when it is yellow. Nope. A truly ripe banana is one that has just begun to get brown freckles or spots on the peel. This is the best, most flavorful, and healthiest time to eat a banana. Store your bananas on your counter top away from other produce, because bananas give off a gas (ethylene) as they ripen, which could affect the ripening process of your other produce. And, if you have a lot of bananas, split them up. This will help prevent all of your bananas from ripening at once. Another great tip for bananas is to freeze them once they're ripe. All you have to do is peel the banana and freeze it in a Ziploc bag, pushing out as much air as possible. When you are ready to use it, take it out and let it thaw for about ten minutes. Frozen bananas are best used in Raw ice creams or smoothies. It also allows you to buy in bulk when prices are good.

- Avocados: Keep avocados on the counter until they reach ripeness. To achieve quicker ripening they can be placed in a loosely closed paper bag with a tomato. When ripe, their skin is usually brown in color and if you gently squeeze it, it gives just a little. Once they're ripe, store them in the refrigerator where they'll last up to a week longer. If you just keep them on the counter, they'll only last another couple of days. Avocados, like bananas, give off a gas, which could affect the ripening process of your other produce, so let them ripen away from your other produce. And, if you have a lot of avocados, split them up. This will help prevent all of your avocados from ripening at the same time.

- Tomatoes: These are best stored on your counter top. These also give off the same gas (ethylene) as bananas and avocados. Do not put them in the refrigerator or they will get a "mealy" texture. To make them last as long as possible, I store mine gently sandwiched between two paper towels (one above, one below) on a glass plate. Tomatoes also freeze quite well if you're going to thaw them for use in a soup or marinara, but not to thaw and eat plain, such as in a salad. If you buy a bunch at once because they're on sale, then you can freeze them when you get home from the store. It's easy. All you do is gently wash the tomatoes, dry them, and place them in plastic bags with as much of the air pushed out as possible. Then make sure the bag is closed tightly (twist tie or Ziploc) and freeze.

- Pineapple: You know pineapple is ripe, at peak sweetness, and ready for eating when you can no longer lift a pineapple by one of its leaves without the leaf coming off. Therefore, test your pineapple for ripeness at the store to ensure you're buying the sweetest one possible. Just start pulling on the leaves. After 3 to 4 attempts on different leaves, if you can't gently take one of them out, then move on to another pineapple.

- Stone fruits (peaches, plums, nectarines, apricots, etc.): If ripe, these will "give" a little when gently pressed. If they are hard, they aren't ripe yet.

146

- Stone fruits, bananas and avocados continue to ripen after being picked. (Cherries do not. Store them in your refrigerator and handle them carefully to avoid bruising.)

- I have produce ripening all over my house. Sounds silly maybe, but I don't want it crowded on my kitchen counter top. I move it around and turn it over daily. Again, ripening fruits give off gas that may affect other produce, so it may be a good idea to keep them separate.

- Mangos: The skin of mangos can be toxic for some people, because it is part of the poison ivy family. You can tell if you are sensitive to it from simply touching the skin and seeing if you get a rash or any skin irritation. Even if you do get a rash from touching it, most people who are sensitive to the skin of a mango can still eat the fruit inside with no problem. I usually keep green, firm kent mangos on my counter for a few days to ripen. When they start to turn in spots (red and yellow) and they "give" a little when pressed, I move them to the refrigerator. A perfect ripe mango will have a nice, intense fragrance.

- Apples: These should be firm to hard. Cold temperatures keep apples from continuing to ripen after they are picked, so you can keep them on your counter for a few days and then move them to the refrigerator.

- Kiwi: You can eat the whole fruit with the skin. Personally, I cut the skin off because I cannot seem to get past the "furriness" of it, but some people eat the whole thing, skin and all. The best kiwis are plump, fragrant and they yield to gentle pressure. Unripe kiwis have a hard core and a very tart taste. To ripen firm kiwis, set them out in room temperature for a few days. To accelerate the process, place them in a paper bag with an apple or banana.

- Citrus: Lemons can be stored at room temperature for up to two weeks without refrigeration. Limes however, should be refrigerated because they are more perishable. Oranges can be kept in the refrigerator or stored at room temperature.

- Pears: These should look relatively unblemished with nice full color. In some varieties, full color will not develop until the fruit ripens. Ripe pears will give a little to gentle pressure. Pears are picked unripe and they are usually hard. Pears can be stored at room temperature first to ripen, then refrigerated for no longer than a day or two before eating them.

- Persimmons: Look for deeply colored fruits, which should be more reddish than yellow. Buy glossy, well rounded persimmons that are free of cracks or bruises, with their leaf-like "sepals" still green and attached. You can leave unripe persimmons at room temperature in a paper bag with an apple to accelerate the process. Ripe persimmons should be stored in the refrigerator, and used as soon as possible.

- Figs: Good figs are plump, unbruised, have a mild fragrance and the skin should not be broken. Ripe fresh figs should be kept in the refrigerator.

- Berries: Do not wash berries until you are ready to eat them. They should always be stored in the refrigerator. Blueberries can last up to a week, but raspberries should usually be eaten within a day or two of purchasing. You can freeze berries as a way to have them year round. You can freeze fresh cranberries for up to a year—unwashed, in freezing bags or glass mason jars. Raspberries and blackberries should be washed before freezing, drained well, then spread out on a baking sheet with wax paper. Freeze until solid, then transfer to a heavy plastic bag or glass mason jar. They can be kept for up to a year.

- Dates: Fresh dates should be somewhat smooth-skinned, glossy, plump and soft; they should not be deeply wrinkled, leathery, broken, or cracked. They can be stored in the refrigerator in glass mason jars to prevent them from absorbing odors from other foods, which dates are known to do. They will last for up to eight months.

- Herbs: Dehydrating herbs yourself is really easy... talk about healthy and full flavor! All you have to do is wash your fresh herbs, dry them with a paper towel, and dehydrate them until thoroughly dry. If you're using an Excalibur dehydrator, it is also helpful to place a mesh screen on top of the herbs while drying. When they are almost completely dry, they'll be super light in weight and the mesh screen ensures they won't fly around inside the dehydrator as the air blows. Store the whole dried leaves in a glass mason jar and take them out as needed. When you are ready to use them, crush the leaves with your fingers, or use a mortar and pestle, for whatever amount you need. Do not crush more than you need; it's best to store dehydrated herbs in the whole leaf form to maintain the fullest flavor.

- Storing fresh herbs: The drier the leaves, the longer and fresher they will keep, so don't wash them before you store them. The best way to store fresh herbs is to put them into a plastic bag (Ziploc, etc.) or packed loosely in a glass mason jar, and keep them at 40 to 45 degrees F, which is typically the temperature in your refrigerator's crisper. I like to keep different varieties in separate bags. Keep herbs in the vegetable crisper or on a refrigerator shelf. It's wise to avoid cold spots like the rear of the lower shelf. If the herbs are just harvested, then most of them should remain in good shape for well over a week, although their intensity of flavor fades over time. Herbs with tough leaves like rosemary, thyme, and sage can keep for two weeks or more.

- I use Evert Green Fresh bags (available in your produce aisle) to store certain items in my refrigerator, such as bell peppers, cucumbers, celery, carrots, apples, lettuce (if it's not pre-bagged) and more.

SWEETENERS TO USE

The following is a list of sweeteners that you might see used in my recipes. It's important to know that the healthiest sweeteners are fresh whole fruits, including fresh dates. That said, dates sometimes compromise texture. As a chef, I look for great texture (which sometimes rules out dates), but as a health food advocate, I lean towards fresh dates whenever possible, so there is a compromise, meaning the best sweetener to use (dates, vs., say agave nectar—which is still pretty healthy) depends on the situation and what you're trying to accomplish (your goals for your daily routine are different than when bringing a dessert to a holiday party, for instance). As a consultant helping people embrace a Raw food lifestyle, I'm very supportive of helping them transition, which sometimes means using agave nectar (or some other sweetener) because it is easy to use, even though, strictly speaking, it might not be quite as healthy as dates. Unless you're very advanced or a purist, both of these are so much healthier than most sweeteners used in the Standard American Diet that it's probably splitting hairs.

Most of my recipes can use pitted dates in place of agave nectar. (Honey is not considered vegan.) There is some debate among Raw food enthusiasts as to whether agave nectar is Raw. The company I use (Madhava®) claims to be Raw and says they don't heat their Raw agave nectar above 118 degrees. If however, your still want to eat the healthiest of sweeteners, then skip the agave nectar and use pitted dates. In most recipes, you can simply substitute 1-2 pitted date(s) for 1 tablespoon of agave nectar. Dates won't give you a super creamy texture, but the texture can be improved by making "date paste" (pureeing, pitted, and soaked dates, with their soak water, in a food processor fitted with the "S" blade). This, of course, takes a little extra time.

If using agave nectar is easier and faster for you, then go ahead and use it; just be sure to buy the Raw version that says it isn't heated above 118 degrees (see KristensRaw.com/store for links to this product). Even though dates are the healthier options, most of my recipes call for agave nectar because that is most convenient for people.

Agave Nectar

There are a variety of agave nectars on the market, but again, not all of them are Raw. Make sure it is labeled "Raw" on the bottle as well as claiming that it isn't processed above 118 degrees. Agave nectar is noteworthy for having a low glycemic index.

Dates

Dates are probably the healthiest of sweeteners, because they're a fresh whole food. Feel free to use dates instead of agave in these recipes. If a recipe calls for 1/4 cup of agave, then you can substitute with approximately 4-6 pitted dates. You can also make your own date sugar by dehydrating pitted dates and then grinding them down. This is a great alternative to Rapadura.®

Honey

Most honey is technically raw, but it is not vegan by most definitions of "vegan" because it is produced by animals, who therefore are at risk of being mistreated. While honey does not have the health risks associated with animal byproducts such as eggs or dairy, it can spike the body's natural sugar levels. Agave nectar has a lower, healthier glycemic index and can replace any recipe you find that calls for honey, in a 1 to 1 ratio.

Maple Syrup

Maple syrup is made from boiled sap of the maple tree. It is not Raw, but some people still use it as a sweetener.

Rapadura®

This is a dried sugarcane juice, and it's not Raw. It is, however, an unrefined and unbleached organic whole-cane sugar. It imparts a nice deep sweetness to your recipes, even if you only use a little. Feel free to omit it if you'd like to adhere to a strictly Raw program. You can substitute Rapadura with home-made date sugar (see Dates above).

Stevia

This is from the leaf of the stevia plant. It has a sweet taste but it doesn't have any calories and doesn't elevate blood sugar levels. It's very sweet, so use much less stevia than you would any other sweetener. My mom actually grows her own stevia. It's a great addition in fresh smoothies, for example, to add some sweetness without the calories. You can use the liquid, white powder, or green powder (this is the least refined) version from the store, but these are not Raw. When possible, the best way to have stevia is grow it yourself.

Yacon Syrup

This sweetener has a low glycemic index, making it very attractive to some people. It has a molasses-like flavor that is nice and rich. You can replace agave and honey with this sweetener in my recipes, but make sure to get the Raw variety, which I've only seen available at www.NaturalZing.com. They offer a few different yacon syrups, including one in particular that is not heat-treated.

LET'S TALK ABOUT STORAGE

The Food Saver

Here is one of the best tips ever for Raw food: Get a Food Saver® and make your life a million times easier with Raw food prep. This is more than just a "food" saver, it's a life saver! I love my Food Saver because it adds a longer shelf life to Raw food. When I make a soup that would normally last three days, I use my Food Saver and I now have a shelf life that is longer... up to a week (they say it'll last much longer than that, I just always end up eating the food before I can see how long it could actually last). I do this with salad dressings, soups, desserts, fresh juices, smoothies, sauces and much more. It's best to use glass mason jars for this, so you'll need the mason jar attachment from Food Saver, which you can find online at FoodSaver.com. The Food Saver is also great for heavier foods of all consistencies, like pesto, burgers, breads and crackers. I can't say enough about how fantastic this tool is in your kitchen. With the Food Saver, you can make extra batches of things and "Food Saver" them so they last longer, meaning you can spend less time in the kitchen.

Glass Mason Jars

I store as much as I can in glass mason jars. It is better for the environment and a much healthier alternative to plastic, which has chemicals that seep into the food. They are inexpensive and can be found at most hardware stores and grocery stores. My dried spices and dried herbs are kept on top of my stove in glass containers. My nuts, seeds and dried unsweetened coconut are stored in glass jars in the freezer. My Raw breads and crackers are stored in the freezer, if I don't plan on eating them within two weeks of making them. I store my dates, raisins and other dried fruits in my refrigerator. It's a smart idea to label everything with the contents and the date… trust me, you WILL forget. You can write on glass mason jars with permanent marker by Sharpie® and it easily scrubs off with a little dish soap and a sponge. Buy a few dozen inexpensive mason jars. You'll want a range of sizes. One-cup, quart, and half gallon-sized mason jars and lids (wide-mouthed) are the best.

YOUR NEW RAW FOOD KITCHEN

Isn't this all exciting? More fun to come, because now I'll teach you about getting the proper equipment for your new Raw food kitchen. It all starts with freedom from the stove. And, oh what a freedom that is! In fact, my oven and microwave are both used for storage. And, my stove has a glass table top on top of it (from an old end table I no longer used), where I set all of my spices and seasonings. This way, they're always out and in sight for me to use. I like to keep all of my equipment on my counter, as well as my seasonings and herbs, so that they are ready for me to use and I don't forget about them. Every time I walk through my kitchen and I see my things, I am reminded of my healthy Raw lifestyle and I get excited because I feel proud and dedicated to have these great tools and equipment. They are also a fun

154

conversation starter when people visit. People are always intrigued by my kitchen and I love demonstrating the equipment for them so they can sample Raw goodies right then and there! That's how I get them hooked! *Shhhhhh... don't tell.* ☺

For outfitting a complete kitchen, I've provided a list of everything I recommend. If I recommended it, I've used it personally. If you end up getting it all, you will have a Raw food kitchen just like I do. The more you get, the easier Raw food prep will be for you, it's that simple. However, like I've said before and I'll say again... baby steps are important and perfectly okay if that's how you'd prefer to proceed. So, take your time transforming your kitchen (if you need to) so that you can get quality equipment that will last you years and years. Set yourself up for success and for fun! For the most preferred and recommended brands I use myself, everything I have listed below can be found online via links on my Web site, KristensRaw.com/store.

Essential Kitchen Equipment

The following tools are listed in order of importance. After this list of essentials, you will see a second list that shows things you'll want in your new Raw food kitchen as soon as you can get them (many of these things you might already have, so check them off if you do).

Chef's Knife

The thing you will be doing the most when prepping Raw food is... chopping. Get a fantastic chef's knife. I cannot emphasize this enough. The brand I prefer and use at home is MAC. A great place to start is a knife that is 6-8 inches in length. Along with this, get an inexpensive knife sharpener. After you sharpen your knife, do the paper test on it. Hold up a piece of paper in one hand and see if your knife can cut it from top to bottom with ease. Be careful, of course.

Additionally, I recommend getting a good paring knife soon after you have your chef's knife.

I also love my ceramic knives and have a couple of them myself. Ceramic knives prevent oxidation of the foods you cut. They are extremely sharp and almost never need sharpening. They are fragile though, so you have to be extra, extra careful with them. That being said, they really rock! They are razor sharp and make you feel like you're cutting room temperature butter with almost anything you cut. I do not use my ceramic knives on hard root vegetables because of the knives' frailty; so that's why I have both the stainless steal Mac and Kyocera Ceramic knives for different uses in my kitchen.

Blender (preferably high-powered)

When you are starting out, you can use any blender. As you start making more Raw foods with nuts and seeds, it will be very helpful to have a high-powered blender. My first choice is the brand Blendtec and my second choice is Vitamix. I have both of these and I always use my Blendtec first. It's easier to clean and scrape the food out, it has a digital display and panel, it fits neatly on my counter (under the cupboard), and it's fantastic. Vitamix is excellent as well, but I prefer the Blendtec for the reasons mentioned above.

Food Processor

A 12 or 14-cup is the best choice, because you will end up using the extra capacity. I also highly recommend getting the extra discs when you can (1mm, 2mm, fine, shredding). I like both Cuisinart and Kitchen Aid brands.

Juicer

If you are going to juice a lot, which I highly recommend if you're looking for the highest health possible, then I recommend getting an excellent juicer. The brand I prefer is the Green Star. It also juices wheatgrass, so you don't need to buy a separate wheat grass juicer. The twin gears used to extract the juice maintain the integrity of the nutrients and enzymes so the juice does not oxidize immediately. This way, you can make a juice and store it in the refrigerator for the day (even 2-3 days studies show). If you use the centrifugal type juicer, you have to drink it immediately after juicing or it oxidizes, losing its anti-oxidant power.

Dehydrator

Excalibur is by far the best manufacturer of consumer dehydrators. I highly recommend buying the 9-tray model instead of the 5-tray because you'll end up using all 9-trays. Trust me. There are so many things you can make with a dehydrator. Make sure you also get the paraflex non-stick sheets for each tray. For some great tips on using your dehydrator, I recommend my book, *Kristen Suzanne's EASY Raw Vegan Dehydrating*, available at KristensRaw.com.

Spiralizer or the Benriner Turning Slicer

You will use this handy tool to make vegetable pasta. The Spiralizer is a "must have" for your Raw food kitchen. It is less expensive than the Benriner Turning Slicer. However, the Benriner Turning Slicer offers you different blades to make a few different size noodles. Benriner is of higher quality, too. I like them both, and prefer the Benriner Turning Slicer because there is more you can do with it. However, I have both and they both work great, they just serve slightly different purposes.

Food Saver

Get a Food Saver® and make your life easier with food prep because you will be able to spend less time in the kitchen. I love my Food Saver because it adds shelf life to Raw food. With the Food Saver, you can make extra batches of things and vacuum seal them, making them last much longer.

V-Slicer and/or Mandolin

I recommend getting both a V-slicer (handheld model) and a mandolin. They are used for making thinly sliced foods (such as ravioli from beets). The mandolin is typically more expensive, but it ensures that you have very evenly sliced foods, it's much easier to control, and you can usually work faster with it. The mandolin is also ideal for larger quantities of foods. The V-slicer is great for foods that you don't care if they're perfectly and evenly sliced and it's good for slicing small quantities.

Travel Blender

If you travel, I highly recommend getting a great little travel blender. In fact, it's a great tool to have in your office, too. Powerful, easy to clean, and portable. My favorite is the Tribest Personal Blender (PB-100).

Extras to Have in Your Fabulous Raw Kitchen

Hand grater for shredding carrots or beets
Fine zester/grater (microplane)
2 bamboo cutting boards*
Hand citrus juicer
Vegetable peeler
Kitchen scissors
Mason Jars of various sizes (wide mouth)
V-shaped dish rack for draining sprouts
Bamboo sushi mat
Vegetable scraper for the cutting board

Garlic press
Kitchen scale
Cheesecloth
2-4 colanders of different sizes
Fine mesh strainer
Spreading spatula (offset) large and small
Spring form pan(s) of different sizes (round and square)
Funnel
Spice (coffee) grinder
Tart pan and pie dish
Square glass baking dish (8x8 inch)
Rubbermaid mixing spatulas of different sizes
Salad spinner
2 and 4-cup size liquid measuring cups
Green produce bags (Evert-Fresh®)
2 sets measuring spoons
2 sets measuring cups
Tomato "shark" for efficiently removing the top of the tomato (it also de-stems strawberries very well)
1-2 squeeze bottles for sauces
Tongs
6 nested mixing bowls
Nut milk bags
Mesh screening and rubber bands to use for mason jars when sprouting**
Lots of great serving dishes to present your food and eat from.

*The reason for two cutting boards is to use one for savory foods (garlic, onions, ginger, etc) and the other board for everything else. Make sure you clean your boards after every use to keep them free of odor. Mark the board for savory and mark the board for sweet so they don't get mixed up. I prefer bamboo because it has a tighter grain and has less chance of harboring bacteria (they look great, too). Always use a towel (damp if necessary) laid flat between the counter surface and the bottom of the bamboo board so the board doesn't slide when you're cutting on it. Alternatively, you can use a tacky mat or even damp paper towel.

**They also sell sprouting jar lids (with wire mesh) designed to fit wide mouth mason jars. You can find these online or sometimes at your local health food store.

PROPER DEHYDRATION TECHNIQUES

Dehydrating your Raw food at a low temperature is a technique that warms and dries the food without diminishing its nutritional integrity.

When using a dehydrator, it is usually recommended that you begin the dehydrating process at a temperature of 140 degrees for 1-2 hours. Then, lower the temperature to 105 degrees for the remaining time of dehydration. Using a high temperature such as 140 degrees, *in the initial stages of dehydration*, does not destroy the nutritional value of the food because, during this initial phase, the food does the most "sweating" (releasing moisture), which cools the food in the same way that sweat cools us when we exercise. Therefore, while the temperature of the air circulating *around* the food is about 140 degrees, the food itself is much cooler. These directions apply only when using an Excalibur Dehydrator because of their Horizontal-Airflow Drying System. Furthermore, I am happy to only recommend Excalibur dehydrators because of their first-class products and customer service.

For more great tips and recipes using your dehydrator, I recommend my book, *Kristen Suzanne's EASY Raw Vegan Dehydrating*, available at KristensRaw.com.

WHAT IS THE DIFFERENCE BETWEEN CHOPPED, DICED, AND MINCED?

Chop

This gives relatively uniform cuts, but doesn't need to be perfectly neat or even. You'll often be asked to chop something before putting it into a blender or food processor, which is why it doesn't have to be uniform size since it'll be getting blended or pureed.

Dice

This produces a nice cube shape, and can be different sizes, depending on which you prefer. This is great for vegetables.

Mince

This produces an even, very fine cut, typically used for fresh herbs, onions, garlic and ginger.

Julienne

This is a fancy term for long, rectangular cuts.

MAJOR TIME-SAVING TIPS

I typically do a lot of these on Sunday, for the week ahead. Juice your lemons for the week and keep the fresh juice in a mason jar in your fridge. Another great tip is to freeze your fresh-squeezed lemon juice in ice cube trays for 24 hours. Then, pop out the frozen lemon juice cubes and store in a zip lock bag or a glass mason jar in the freezer. Whenever you need some lemon juice, take out a few cubes to thaw. It's also fun and delicious to add the frozen lemon juice cubes to plain water. I do the same thing with my watermelon smoothie. I freeze it in ice cube trays and use them to flavor and "chill" my ordinary water to sass it up. ☺

Crush a head or two of garlic and keep it in a little jar with some olive oil drizzled on it. This saves you a little bit of time so you don't have to continuously press garlic and then clean the garlic press. Do it every few days and that's it.

Use your calendar to plan. Look at some recipes you want to make to see if nuts or seeds need to be soaked (and/or soaked and dehydrated). When you make the recipe, you literally just put the ingredients into a blender or food processor. Voila!

I keep a lot of nuts and seeds already soaked and dehydrated in my freezer. This way, I have them ready for recipes calling for them in that form. Make your life easier... buy a bunch of nuts and seeds and spend one day a month or every few weeks to soak them and dehydrate them. See directions, below.

Make fresh green and/or fruit smoothies three days a week. Make enough for two days each time, and store them in glass mason jars with the lids tightly secured. Fill them as much as you can, allowing as little air as possible remaining in there. If you have the Food Savor and mason jar attachment, then you're all set... use it. Shake it up before drinking.

SOAKING AND DEHYDRATING NUTS AND SEEDS

This is an important topic. When using most nuts and seeds in Raw foods, you'll find that recipes sometimes call for them to be "soaked" or "soaked and dehydrated." Here is the low-down on the importance of it and the difference.

Why should you soak your nuts and seeds? Most nuts and seeds come packed by Mother Nature with enzyme inhibitors, rendering them harder to digest. By soaking your nuts and seeds, you will release and break down the enzyme inhibitors, greatly enhancing the nuts' digestibility. Soaking is highly recommended if you want to experience Raw food in the healthiest way possible. You'll need a dehydrator for this. If you don't' have one yet, then, if a recipe calls for "soaked and dehydrated," just use the nuts or seeds in the form that you bought them at the store (as is).

Some nuts and seeds don't have to follow the enzyme inhibitor rule; therefore, they don't need to be soaked. These are:

• macadamia nuts

- hemp seeds

- brazil nuts

- pine nuts

- cashews (most brands)

An additional note... there are times when the recipe will call for soaking, even though it's for a type of nut without enzyme inhibitors, such as pine nuts. The logic behind this is to help *soften* the nuts so they blend into a smoother texture, especially if you don't have a high-powered blender. This is helpful when making nut milks, soups and sauces.

Some recipes call for "soaked and dehydrated" nuts or seeds. While it might seem pointless to soak something and then dry it, the rationale for this is that some recipes need a "dry" nut texture, almost like a flour. Since the nuts have already been "soaked," the enzyme inhibitor has been broken down for easier digestion. And then they're dehydrated, which gives a "dry" texture. The only way to accomplish this, in the healthiest fashion, is to use a dehydrator. This is a great thing to do before storing your nuts and seeds in the freezer or refrigerator (preferably in glass mason jars). They will last a long time and you'll always have them on hand, ready to use.

With respect to my recipes, I always use "soaked and dehydrated" nuts and seeds, unless otherwise stated with soaking directions.

Directions for "Soaking" and "Soaking & Dehydrating" Nuts

Soaking

The general rule to follow: Any nuts or seeds that require soaking can be soaked overnight (6-10 hours). Put the required amount of nuts or seeds into a bowl and add enough water to cover. Set them on your counter overnight. The following morning, or 6-10 hours after you soaked them, drain and rinse them. Now, they're ready to eat or use in a recipe. At this point, they need to be refrigerated in an airtight container (preferably a glass mason jar) and they'll have a shelf life of about 3 days maximum. Only soak the amount you're going to need or eat, unless you plan on dehydrating them right away.

A note about flax seeds and chia seeds: These don't need to be soaked if your recipe calls for grinding them into a powder. Some recipes will call to soak them in their "whole-seed" form, before making crackers and bread, because they create a very gelatinous and binding texture when soaked. You can soak flax or chia seeds in a ratio of one part seeds to two parts water, and they can be soaked for as short as 2 hours and up to 12 hours. At this point, they are ready to use (you don't drain them). Personally, when I use flax seeds, I usually grind them and don't soak them. It's hard for your body to digest "whole" flax seeds, even if they are soaked, but much easier for your body to assimilate the nutrients, when they're ground to a flax meal.

Soaking & Dehydrating:

Follow the same directions for soaking. Then, after draining and rinsing the nuts, spread them out on a mesh dehydrator sheet and dehydrate them at 140 degrees for one hour. Lower the temperature to 105 degrees and dehydrate them until they're completely dry, which can take up to 24 hours.

MEASUREMENT CONVERSIONS

1 tablespoon = 3 teaspoons
1 ounce = 2 tablespoons
1/4 cup = 4 tablespoons
1/3 cup = 5 1/3 tablespoons

1 cup
= 8 ounces
= 16 tablespoons
= 1/2 pint

1/2 quart
= 1 pint
= 2 cups

1 gallon
= 4 quarts
= 8 pints
= 16 cups
= 128 ounces

CHAPTER 14

WHERE ARE YOU TODAY?

Everyone knows that we should be eating fresh whole foods, like fruits and vegetables, right? It's no secret that most people need more of these in their diet. With Raw cuisine, it's never been more exciting! We're not limited to just carrot and celery sticks anymore. I promise that you will look forward to your Raw fruits and vegetables (like never before), because they taste great.

Identify where you are today in your dietary habits and lifestyle, and then use the information below to figure out your next steps with respect to living your new Raw lifestyle. Implement the suggestions and you'll be on your way to superior health. You don't need to dive straight into 100% Raw. Some people go "High Raw," which means you're about 75-99% Raw. See what makes you feel the healthiest and go from there.

The first thing to remember... don't limit yourself with how much Raw food you eat. Just eat what you need and what you feel is natural. Your body will guide you. This is really important in the beginning to ensure your success, so you don't feel deprived. Deprivation is one of the biggest reasons people fail on diets. In only a short period of time, I felt fewer cravings and was completely satisfied with my new lifestyle. Now I have days where I only want fruits and vegetables and other days when I want nut pates and dessert. It's an exciting evolution, so embrace it, enjoy it, and take it one day, week or month at a time. Be flexible to make changes and listen to your body.

The next step is to reduce or eliminate unhealthy food from your diet. This includes junk food, packaged and processed snacks, animal-based products, fried foods, white sugar, and white flour. Here is the fun part: Go through your cabinets and throw these junk foods away. Don't say, "I'll just eat these this last time so I don't waste them." NO! Throw this junk out! Ceremoniously, if you like. (Bonfire, anyone?) Your life is changing. You are on a new path to optimal health. When I did this, I cranked up the soundtrack from the movie "Rocky" and filled my ears with "Eye of the Tiger" and it totally pumped me up. I threw that junk food into the trash with ferocity (because it was "junk" after all!). Then, I took a picture of the garbage in my trash can so I would remember it as that... garbage.

PLAN OF ATTACK

One option is to go cold turkey (if this is you, then great!). Going cold turkey was not something I wanted to do because I had to get off caffeine, which was a gradual process in my case. Again, whatever works for you.

Another option is having a nice transition period to the Raw lifestyle. When taking this approach, you can do it one of two ways:

1) Split *each day* between Raw meals and non-Raw meals. This means that maybe you'll have a Raw breakfast and lunch but a cooked vegan dinner. Or, you'll have Raw food and cooked food at each meal, gradually increasing the amount of Raw food until you're either High Raw (75-99% Raw) or 100% Raw.

2) The other option is to have certain days of the week where you eat 100% Raw and other days of the week where you eat part Raw and part cooked vegan. This is what worked best for me so I'm going to go into detail for that plan.

IF YOU ARE NEW TO RAW...

Start out by picking one day a week (or more if you want) to eat 100% Raw all day long. You'll see how easy it is and how amazing you feel. You'll soon be excited to do more than one day a week, maybe two to three days. After that, start increasing to one week straight, then two weeks, then up to a month (leaving a little wiggle room here and there, for times you just "can't" do it, perhaps due to social situations). Find what works for you.

It's important to write your plan for going Raw on your calendar. Planning it and putting it in writing is one the best ways to help you accomplish your goal so you don't get off track. On the days you're 100% Raw, write "*100% Raw - no exceptions*" on that day. On the days that your goal *is not* to be 100% Raw, simply start adding more Raw foods to your daily food choices. For example, maybe you commit to three days of 100% Raw and four days of 50% Raw (don't let the other 50% cooked be junk or processed foods though—pick something that is still relatively healthy... and be sure to stay vegan). Some people do this by eating a salad before lunch and dinner or having their traditional cooked vegetable side dishes made from Raw food instead (and then having only the main entree be cooked). Or, some people start by having a piece of fruit before their normal cooked breakfast, for example. Another option is to have a cooked dinner, but have Raw breakfast and lunch on the days that you are not 100% Raw.

And remember, if you fall off the wagon, don't worry, just get right back on. Every minute of every day is a chance to start anew!

EATING ARTFULLY, GLAMOROUSLY, AND HEALTHFULLY

We feast with our eyes first because we look at what we eat before we eat it. If something looks good, then we are inclined to believe that it will taste good. This is where Raw food is especially easy because it's full of beautiful, radiant and vibrant colors from the health giving phytonutrients. A rainbow a day in my food is what I aim to accomplish.

To take your meals to the next level of enjoyment, make your eating experience the best ever with the help of a simple, gorgeous and glamorous presentation. As mentioned earlier, it's always *location, location, location* with real estate, and *presentation, presentation, presentation* with food. I use my best dishes when I eat. I use beautiful wine glasses for my smoothies and juices. I use fancy goblets for many of my desserts. Why? Because I'm worth it. And, so are you! Nothing makes plain water taste better than a sexy, beautiful wine glass from which to sip. Don't save your good china just for company. Believe me, you'll notice the difference. Eating well is an attitude, and when you take care of yourself, your body will respond in kind.

CHAPTER 15

TRAVEL IN THE RAW

Travel can be the result of many things. For some people, travel is associated with vacationing, which is supposed to be relaxing and fun. Some people travel for work. Some people have to travel last minute due to emergencies. It doesn't matter what the reason is for the travel, people living the Raw lifestyle usually have the same concern: How to stay Raw while traveling.

Bottom line: It's very much about being prepared. When going on vacation, if you have the time to plan a few things in advance, your ability to stay Raw while you travel will be that much easier. And, for those times that you have to pack and leave quickly, it's always nice to have a few things on hand, know where they are, and grab them on your way out the door. *(The purpose of this travel section is mainly to give information about staying Raw while traveling throughout the United States.)*

I have organized this chapter into four parts:

- Car trips — short (day trips, possibly overnight)

- Car trips — long (a weekend or longer)

- Airplane trips — short (one week or less)*

- Airplane trips — long (longer than a week)*

Obvious things to keep in mind... if you're able to get fresh organic food on your trip, then you should bank on that and not pack as much. Pack enough for the day until you can buy some fresh produce. This applies to trips in the car where you're driving for days or trips where you fly. Check your destination on the Web for locations of Whole Foods, Sprouts, Trader Joes, Sunflower Market, local farmer's markets and some of your other favorites that carry organic produce. Then, you can mark them on your map for traveling.

NOTE: There are deliberate redundancies in the following four travel scenarios so that, in the future, you can just skip to the scenario that matches your immediate travel situation.

1. CAR TRIPS – SHORT (DAY TRIPS, POSSIBLY OVERNIGHT)

For short car trips you basically need a medium size cooler, Ziploc bags doubled up with ice to keep the cooler cold. Then, as it melts, you can dump out the melt-water and refresh it with ice from fast food restaurants, gas station soda pop machines, or ice machines at your hotel. You'll also want some snacks and a few other things (hopefully you'll be able to find sources for fresh organic produce while on your trip—see note above about finding these sources ahead of time).

Raw Travel Kit

- 1 large Ziploc baggie of salad mix, ready to eat
- 1 container of salad dressing already made
- Wooden plate or bowl
- Small flexible chopping mat
- Knife with protective case
- Beverage container with watertight lid (filled with water)

- 1 or more small containers of granola, dried fruit, nuts, snacks
- Apples (or other firm fruit with skin)
- Green Smoothie
- Plastic bags for trash and compost
- Kitchen towel and sponge, bio-degradable cleanser (travel size)
- Enzymes (if you end up eating cooked vegan food, these can help digest the food)
- Forks

2. CAR TRIPS – LONG (A WEEKEND OR LONGER)

For longer trips, you basically need to make a portable kitchen. You need a large cooler, if possible, with Ziploc bags doubled up with ice to keep the cooler cold. Then, as it melts, you can dump it out and refresh it with ice from fast food restaurants, gas station soda pop machines, or ice machines at the hotel you stay at. You also want some snacks and a few other things (hopefully you'll be able to find sources for fresh organic produce while on your trip—see note above about finding these sources ahead of time).

Here is a *great tip...* get online and order fresh whole organic food to be delivered to your travel destination. It'll cost you a few extra bucks, but it's worth it! Why? Because you're worth it! *Diamondorganics.com* or *boxedgreens.com* are great places to start and they will typically deliver right to your hotel room or wherever you are staying. Also, you can order from places such as NaturalZing.com for some treats (flax crackers, cookies, etc.)... and why not? You're on vacation, right? Spend the extra few bucks to have healthy food shipped to where you're going if you're going to be there for a while. Or, order a few days of Raw meals from RAWvolution.com and PureRawCafe.com, delivered to your destination if you're staying somewhere with a refrigerator or cooler.

Alternatively, you can just bring some Raw treats (cookies, crackers, trail mix, granola, etc.) because they pack well and last a while.

Lightweight blender – I like the Tribest Personal Blender (PB-100 Blending Package with S-blade assembly, available on my website: *KristensRaw.com/store*).

Raw Travel Kit

- Wooden plate(s) or bowl(s)
- Small flexible chopping mat
- Knife with protective case
- Vegetable peeler
- Beverage container with watertight lid (filled with water)
- 1 or more small containers of granola, dried fruit, nuts, snacks
- Sealable plastic bags of various sizes
- Apples (or other firm fruit with skin)
- Travel blender made of light-weight plastic
- Favorite seasonings and Himalayan crystal salt
- Plastic bags for trash and compost
- Small rubber spatula
- Quick dry table cover (a lightweight sarong works great!)–this really makes it seem like you're more at home, especially if you're in a hotel room, and it's great for picnic-style road trips.
- Kitchen towel and sponge, bio-degradable cleanser (travel size, or purchase when you arrive)
- Nutmilk** or sprouting bag with drawstring for sprouting seeds and/or straining nut milk. Soak seeds in a sprout bag inside a Ziploc (or sink) filled with water. Then remove the sprout bag after 8 hours and hang it in the shower to drain (if using to grow sprouts).

- Plastic produce spinning bag for washing salad greens
- Water for food prep (smoothies, soups, rinsing produce)
- Enzymes (if you end up eating cooked vegan food, these can help digest the food)
- Baby food mill (to make small batches of pate)
- Frozen coconut water or purified water which serves as ice in cooler. Once it's thawed, you drink it.
- Green powder is great for traveling so you can stay green if you can't have your fresh green juices and smoothies.
- Forks

3. AIRPLANE TRIPS – SHORT (1 WEEK OR LESS)*

If you're going by plane, you need enough food in your carry-on to get you through the plane ride, then you need some things in your luggage to make life more Raw friendly once you've arrived at your travel destination. If your trip is a week or less, you might not want to bring everything detailed below. It depends on your destination. If you have local places that you'll be able to enjoy salads and other Raw foods, then you can count on those to feed you most of the time. If not, I would suggest packing some produce in your checked luggage.

Here is a *great tip:* Get online and order fresh whole organic food to be delivered to your travel destination. It'll cost you a few bucks, but it's worth it! Why? Because you're worth it! *Diamondorganics.com* or *boxedgreens.com* are great places to start and they will typically deliver right to your hotel room or wherever you are staying. Also, you can order from places such as NaturalZing.com for some treats (flax crackers, cookies, etc.)... and why not? You're on vacation, right? Spend the extra few bucks to have healthy food shipped to where you're going if you're going to be there for a while. Or, order a few days of Raw meals from RAWvolution.com or PureRawCafe.com, delivered to your destination if you're staying somewhere with a refrigerator or cooler.

Alternatively, you can just bring some Raw treats (cookies, crackers, trail mix, granola, etc.) because they pack well and last a while.

The following can be in your carry-on for the plane ride, and I'd have some in your checked luggage for when you arrive. Airplane trips are tricky because of the new regulations. The safest bet is to take foods like pre-washed apples (or other firm fruit with skin), cucumbers (I eat these like a giant carrot stick), carrots, celery, and small containers of Raw cereal, dried fruit, nuts and snacks.

Raw Travel Kit (for Your Checked Luggage)

- Lightweight blender—I like Tribest Personal Blender (PB-100 Blending Package with S-blade assembly, available on my website: *KristensRaw.com/store*).
- Vegetable peeler
- Wooden plate(s) or bowl(s)
- Favorite seasonings and Himalayan crystal salt
- Small rubber spatula
- Table cover (a lightweight sarong works great!)—This really makes it seem like you're more at home, especially if you're in a hotel room.
- Kitchen towel and sponge, bio-degradable cleanser (travel size, or purchase when you arrive)
- Small jar with lid for shaking dressings
- Enzymes (if you end up eating cooked vegan food, these can help digest the food)
- Green powder—great for traveling so you can stay green if you can't have your fresh green juices and smoothies.
- Forks

4. AIRPLANE TRIPS – LONG (LONGER THAN ONE WEEK)*

If you're going by plane, you need enough food in your carry-on to get you through the plane ride, then you need some things in your luggage to make life more Raw friendly once you've arrived at your travel destination.

Here is a *great tip:* Get online and order fresh whole organic food to be delivered to your travel destination. It'll cost you a few extra bucks, but it's worth it! Why? Because you're worth it! *Diamondorganics.com* or *boxedgreens.com* are great places to start and they will typically deliver right to your hotel room or wherever you are staying. Also, you can order from places such as NaturalZing.com for some treats (flax crackers, cookies, etc.)... and why not? You're on vacation, right? Spend the extra few bucks to have healthy food shipped to where you're going if you're going to be there for a while. Or, order a few days of Raw meals from RAWvolution.com or PureRawCafe.com, delivered to your destination if you're staying somewhere with a refrigerator or cooler.

Alternatively, you can just bring some Raw treats (cookies, crackers, trail mix, granola, etc.) because they pack well and last a while.

The following can be in your carry-on for the plane ride, and I'd have some in your checked luggage for when you arrive. Airplane trips are tricky because of the new regulations. The safest bet is to take foods like pre-washed apples (or other firm fruit with skin), cucumbers (I eat these like a giant carrot stick), carrots, celery, and small containers of Raw cereal, dried fruit, nuts and snacks.

Raw Travel Kit (for Your Checked Luggage)

- Lightweight blender–I like Tribest Personal Blender (PB-100 Blending Package with S-blade assembly, available on my website: *KristensRaw.com/store*).
- Vegetable peeler
- Favorite seasonings and Himalayan crystal salt
- Wooden plate(s) or bowl(s)
- Small rubber spatula
- Table cover (a lightweight sarong works great!)–This really makes it seem like you're more at home, especially if you're in a hotel room.
- Kitchen towel and sponge, bio-degradable cleanser (travel size, or purchase when you arrive)
- Nutmilk** or sprouting bag with drawstring for sprouting seeds and/or straining nut milk. Soak seeds in a sprout bag inside a Ziploc (or sink) filled with water. Then remove the sprout bag after 8 hours and hang it in the shower to drain (if using to grow sprouts).
- Plastic produce spinning bag for washing salad greens
- Enzymes (if you end up eating cooked vegan food, these can help digest the food)
- Baby food mill (to make small batches of pate)
- Green powder is great for traveling so you can stay green if you can't have your fresh green juices and smoothies.
- Forks

Last but not least, if you can't do any of the above... take something with you... a memento. It could be a good luck charm, a ring, a few Raw food bars, a Raw food book, anything. This is to remind you that you live a lifestyle that is high in Raw food. Then, maybe take the vacation time and relax and not worry about staying Raw or organic for the whole duration. Eat cooked vegan food if necessary, but take smaller portions so you don't get addicted. Then, look at this "memento" reminder that you brought with you and say to yourself,

"I live a lifestyle HIGH in Raw food, and this is here to remind me of that. While I'm traveling, I might allow myself to have some cooked food, but when I'm back home, I'll get right back into embracing Raw."

And resume *the day* you get back.

* FTA's rules for air travel security are always changing. If you're taking an airplane for your trip, you may need to make adjustments based on what you are allowed to bring on the airplane with respect to food and liquids.

** This recipe is available in all of my Raw recipe books available at KristensRaw.com.

CHAPTER 16

14-DAY SAMPLE MEAL PLAN

I am asked all the time for a meal plan or what would be a typical 14-days of food in my life. The following represents an example of what you might see me eating. Keep in mind, this changes by the month and season. It's only a sample of random days.

You'll see that I make a lot of food using recipes from my Raw food recipe books (denoted with an "*"). If you don't have these yet, simply replace them with something similar. For example, if I have listed blueberries for a smoothie and you don't like blueberries, then substitute them with raspberries, etc. Or, if I make a pate recipe from one of my books, and you want to use a pate from another book, go right ahead.

THINGS TO NOTE

- Drink plenty of water throughout the day to stay hydrated.

- Every morning, when you wake up, drink 8 ounces of water (warmed, if you like) with the juice of 1/2 or 1 whole lemon. Drink this cleansing tonic while you get ready for your day.

- Drinking fresh vegetable and fruit juice (*"Plant Blood"*) is vital for optimal health. This is where you're going to get loads and loads of vitamins, minerals, phytonutrients and enzymes, all of which are easily absorbed. As Dr. Normal

Walker wrote in his book, *Fresh Vegetable and Fruit Juices*, "Any person not familiar with the nutritional and recuperative value of fresh vegetable and fruit juices is woefully uninformed." Everyone needs to have fresh Plant Blood on a daily basis. Whether you're 100% Raw or 10% Raw, 100% Vegan or 50% Vegan, toddler age or a senior... you need to drink fresh vegetable and fruit juice *every day*. Drinking Plant Blood daily is what divides the men from the boys, the divas from the groupies, and makes all the difference in the world when it comes to ultimate health.

I have listed breakfast, lunch, and dinner in the following plan. If you'd like a snack, then have one. Some great snacks include a green smoothie, or chopped tomatoes & fresh basil drizzled with a little Raw organic olive or hemp oil, or perhaps some diced cucumbers and pineapple, fresh squeezed lime juice and sprinkled with minced cilantro and Himalayan crystal salt.

- When I say big salad, I mean *big salad*. Don't be shy on the amount of lettuce and veggies because you want it *to fill you up*. I usually top it off with 2-4 tablespoons of dressing. One trick is to "water" down the dressing a little... so it spreads over more of the lettuce and veggies and this way you're *flavoring the lettuce*. This can really help when making big salads, while keeping the flavor great and not adding a lot of extra calories from fat.

- Eat until you're full. If the amounts I've presented leave you still hungry, eat more.

- Exercise! I weight train about 3-5 days a week and do cardio 2-3 days. Sometimes both are done in one session, meaning that I might exercise for three days on, one day off, three days on, one day off. For the day off, I still might take an extra long walk with my dog, do a little swimming or simply rest.

If you think you don't have time to exercise, then—some tough love here—you're not yet truly serious about your health. When you're serious about something, you make it a priority, which literally means it comes first ("prior"). To reach optimum health, you must be physically active and fit. Just start somewhere, because a little exercise is better than nothing, and it gets the habit started. It might mean getting up 15 minutes early, with your tennis shoes next to the bed and you sleep in your gym shorts and sport bra (if you're a woman)... then you take a brisk 10-minute walk right when you wake up.

THE MEAL PLAN

Day 1

Breakfast

- Large fresh herb/banana smoothie: 1-2 tablespoons minced herbs (dill, rosemary, and/or basil, etc.) and 2-3 bananas blended with 2 cups of water

Lunch

- Large salad with a Raw dressing, 2 olives, 1 red bell pepper seeded and chopped, 1 cucumber chopped and lots of sprouts

Dinner

- Large portion of Zucchini Pasta with Raw Marinara*

Dessert

- Key Lime Pudding*

Day 2

Breakfast

- Large spinach and apple cinnamon smoothie: 2 handfuls of spinach, 2 cups of water, 2 apples (cored and chopped), 1/4 – 1/2 teaspoon cinnamon

Lunch

- (Left over from yesterday)
- Big portion of Zucchini Pasta Marinara*
- Small version of the salad from yesterday

Dinner

- Raw Hummus* with vegetables (carrots, orange bell pepper slices, celery and cucumber) to dip
- Salad

Dessert

- Key Lime Pudding*

Day 3

Breakfast

- Banana celery smoothie made with 2 cups of water, 2-3 bananas, 2-3 stalks of celery

Lunch

- Large Salad with Raw dressing: 2 cups lettuce, 3 chopped carrots, 1 diced zucchini, 2 stalks celery chopped, 1 medium tomato, chopped. In this salad, I've watered down the dressing a little before putting it on so that it covers more of the veggies, adding flavor, but without adding a lot of fat.

Dinner

- Green smoothie of spinach and banana – a smaller portion because dinner is soon: 1 cup of water, 2 bananas and 1 handful of spinach.
- Hummus from last night with veggie sticks

Day 4

Breakfast

- 1 quart fresh Plant Blood (green juice)

Lunch

- 4 bananas (yes, really)

Snack

- 1/4 cup hemp seeds

Dinner

- Large portion Carrot Pasta with Indian Marinara*
- 1 1/2 cups Kristen Suzanne's Famous Creamed Carrot Soup*

Day 5

Breakfast

- Cilantro mango smoothie: 2 cups water, 2 mangos (peeled and pitted), 1 bunch cilantro

Lunch

- Leftovers from last night's dinner

Snack

- Sesame Seed Candy*

Dinner

- Leftovers from last night's dinner

Day 6

Breakfast

- 3 cups of chunked watermelon

Snack

- 1 quart fresh Plant Blood

Lunch

- Moroccan Gazpacho (free recipe available on my blog at at kristensraw.com—search for "gazpacho")
- Flax crackers (if you don't already have any made, you can buy these at Whole Foods or GoRaw.com)

Dinner

- Green smoothie: 1/2 bunch parsley, 1 banana, and organic edible flowers.
- Beachfront Wrap (a salad wrap sandwich in collard green)*

Dessert

- Orange Blossom Sweet Stuffing*

Day 7

Breakfast

- Blueberry banana smoothie with 2 cups of water, 1 cup of fresh blueberries and 3 bananas.

Lunch

- Kristen Suzanne's Kale Salad*

Dinner

- Kristen Suzanne's Kale salad leftovers from lunch
- Kristen Suzanne's Harvest Soup (free recipe available on my blog, see KristensRaw.com)

Dessert

- Orange Blossom Sweet Stuffing*

Day 8

Breakfast

- Kristen Suzanne's Famous Pancakes with Maple Sauce*

Lunch

- Guacamole and fresh salsa

Dinner

- Guacamole and fresh salsa leftovers from lunch
- Kristen Suzanne's Harvest Soup* leftovers from yesterday

Day 9

Breakfast

- 1 quart fresh Plant Blood

Snack

- Green Smoothie of 2 bananas, 1 cup water, and 1 tablespoon fresh rosemary and 1 tablespoon fresh mint

Lunch

- Zucchini Pasta and Exquisite Cilantro Ginger Pesto*

Dinner

- Large portion of Celery Picnic Salad*

Day 10

Breakfast

- 3 cups of fresh berries: blueberries, strawberries, and blackberries

Snack

- Green Smoothie (any recipe—for ideas, see my recipe books*)

Lunch

- Sauerkraut (Rejuvenative Foods makes a Raw variety, available at Whole Foods)
- Celery Picnic Salad* leftovers from yesterday

Dinner

- Creamy Avocado Breeze Soup*

- Cinnamon Thyme Vegetables*

Dessert

- A Crazy Good Bar*

Day 11

Breakfast

- Vanilla Kiwi Smoothie*

Lunch

- Leftovers from last night's dinner

Dinner

- Chopped carrots, red bell pepper and celery to dip into Cheezy Nacho Sauce*

Dessert

- Green Smoothie with Raw chocolate

Day 12

Breakfast

- 1 quart fresh Plant Blood

Snack

- 1 quart fresh Plant Blood

Lunch

- 2 bananas, 1 peach, 1 cucumber

Dinner

- Chinese Spiced Mushroom Bisque*
- Tahini Garden Medley*

Day 13

Breakfast

- 3 bananas

Lunch

- 2 apples, then wait 25 minutes to eat...
- Chinese Spiced Mushroom Bisque leftover from yesterday

Dinner

- Leftovers from last night's dinner

Day 14

Breakfast

- Fun Chocolate Applesauce*

Lunch

- Zucchini Pasta with Light and Lively Tahini Parsley Dressing drizzled over it*

Dinner

- Seaside Cottage Spread* with a plateful of fresh veggies for dipping

* Recipe available in my Raw recipe books available at KristensRaw.com.

CHAPTER 17

RAW FOR INTERMEDIATES

GETTING YOUR GROOVE ON!

New things begin to happen as you enter this phase of Raw, where you're really "gettin' your groove on." There isn't a specific time for this and I can't say you'll be here in six or nine or twelve months. It depends on how well you progress and how Raw you are. Basically, you're getting very comfortable in your new "Raw skin" lifestyle. By now, your body odor is probably smelling nice (that is, not smelling at all), your breath is sweet (even in the morning), your skin is glowing, and you're feeling better than ever.

TAKING IT TO A NEW LEVEL – FOOD COMBINING

What Is Food Combining? Is It Important?

Food combining refers to eating different kinds of foods separately or together, in such a way so as to facilitate optimal digestion. Your body uses different methods to digest different kinds of food. Some of these processes counteract other processes, such that it would be better if you had eaten those foods at different times.

You want food to move through your system and be assimilated or eliminated as quickly as possible.

It is therefore good to know how to combine foods so that meals require as little time as possible in the digestive system. Correct combinations can assist proper digestion, assimilation, and elimination of each food eaten. You can also experience better sleep when you combine your foods better.

Here are some basics for food combining to get you started. Remember, these are just some basic guidelines. I personally do not follow them strictly. By being mindful of these principles and applying them when you want, you can improve your digestion. For example, if I have a long day ahead of me and I know I'll need a lot of energy, then I follow them more strictly. Also... it's important to note that as your body becomes more and more clean from following the Raw lifestyle, your body changes and handles food combining more efficiently. This is why some people do fine when they're not following strict food combining principles and some don't. Some do better with it after having spent some time eating Raw; others have great success with food combining right away. It is a little different for everyone. Furthermore, if there are some times that you're finding yourself tired more often than not (and it's not a detox stage for you) then you can try following some basic principles to increase your energy and bypass or hasten any lethargy or sluggishness that might accompany digestion of your meals (especially larger meals, or richer foods).

- Rule number one: let your body guide you. The best teacher of all is You, so pay attention to yourself.

- With all apologies to traditional fruit salad... from now on, eat melons alone. Period. It's a good idea to always follow this rule because melons, unlike other fruits, will start to ferment in your system very quickly. That means that if you're eating any melon, don't eat any other type of food within 20 minutes of eating the last bite of melon.

The good news is that melon moves so quickly through your system that it's no problem just 20 minutes later.

- Fruits, in general, digest faster than other foods. Therefore, if you're going to mix fruit with other foods, it's advised to eat the fruit first, try to wait about 30 minutes and then eat the other foods. More specifically, it's optimal to eat "like fruits with like fruits". For example, eat acid fruits with acid fruits, sweet fruits with sweet fruits and sub-acid fruits with sub-acid fruits.

- Drink your liquids between meals, not with meals. Liquids dilute your digestive enzymes and slow digestion.

- Leafy greens pretty much go with everything i.e. fruits, vegetables, nuts, seeds, etc. (except melons, which, again, I always eat separately).

- When possible, for the most part, keep fats and fruits separate. This of course, doesn't apply with gourmet Raw desserts, which usually mix a lot of fat and fruit. Mixing these is not ideal, but it's a heck of a lot better than eating a Snickers any day. There are times when you'll want to be more strict with things like this, such as when you want extra energy, training for an athletic event, recovering from illness or injury, etc.

- For optimal assimilation of vitamins, phyto-chemicals, and minerals, drink your juices alone on an empty stomach, or 30 minutes before other foods.

- Very important: Don't stress about it. Keep it simple and you'll succeed.

CLEANSES

"Cleansing" is a very broad term that refers to giving your digestive system a rest (thus helping it to detoxify) via temporary abstinence of putting certain foods (or all food) into your system. It is also called "fasting." Cleanses/fasts broadly mean you restrict what goes in; they don't necessarily mean you stop eating altogether. For instance, you might cleanse by only eating fruit, or drinking juice, or water, for a period of time.

Cleanses are a great way to keep you in that motivated "Jump Start" frame of mind, like the excitement you have when you first go vegan or Raw. Every few months, I do some sort of fast, which further cleans me out, gives me extra energy and makes me love Raw food all over again. There's nothing that can make you appreciate a simple tomato or piece of lettuce more than having to restrict yourself of eating for a set period of time. It's like that old saying, "You don't know what you got until it's gone." Experiencing true hunger, in all its stages, also can have important psychological, spiritual, and social implications... not the least of which is learning not to take anything for granted. (For these and other symbolic reasons, fasting is an important ritual in many religions.)

The kind of cleanse I do varies. I've done many over the years: the Master Cleanse (very popular, check Google for details); a green juice cleanse; green smoothie cleanse; low fat, whole-food, all fruit cleanse; etc. My cleanses typically range from 1-3 days, occasionally lasting up to 5 days or so.

Some people do them much longer—30 days, or even longer—but I consider such durations to be very advanced. I do not recommend attempting them without first conducting much research, gaining some experience, and consulting with a doctor who is knowledgeable about and comfortable with the basic idea of cleansing.

EXERCISE FOR INTERMEDIATES

It doesn't matter what you eat... you can never be truly healthy unless you are physically fit. Diet does not make your heart strong. It does not make your muscles strong. Nor your bones. All of these require movement and loading (resistance of some form or another). Diet does not remove toxins through your lymp system... movement does this. The list goes on and on. Even higher brain functions (memory, learning, verbal skills, etc.) have consistently been shown to improve with physical exercise. Some studies even demonstrate that physical exercise is more important to brain function than cognitive exercises related to the brain function being measured! In other words, get moving!*

If you're not exercising now, why are you waiting? A more ideal time in your life? Um, that would be NOW. And the rest of your life. (If you don't like the term "exercise" then give it a new moniker... call it "*physical excellence.*") Exercise takes your Raw lifestyle to new heights, so get started!

If you are already exercising, then congratulations. Maybe now is a good time to change it up and keep the momentum going. Join a team, learn a new sport (for example, snowboarding, tennis, or yoga), or try a new gym. Sometimes changing gyms is a great way to get inspired to workout harder and it's fun. You get to meet new people, try new equipment, etc.

* Always check with a physician before starting a physical program.

195

CHAPTER 18

SPROUTING

WHY SPROUT?

"Sprouting" is when you cultivate seeds in a non-soil environment just long enough for them to "wake up" from their dormant stage, burst into life, and sprout little, tiny stems and tiny leaves... *and then you eat 'em!*

Get ready to have fun! Sprouting is one of the best tools you can use to helping you stay on the Raw lifestyle path. I'm going to let you in on a little secret (the gardeners among you might know this already)... aside from the physical/health benefits of eating sprouts (which many people speak about) few people recognize sprouting for what it does to your *mental* outlook. The process of growing your own sprouts is simply *amazing!* When I walk into my kitchen every day and see these little babies growing from seed to fresh sprout, it makes me smile and I'm reminded about the pure, "living" lifestyle I lead... it's impossible to miss it, because these little foods are growing and sprouting before my eyes. It inspires me and I reflect on the clean, pure, fresh, and green lifestyle I've chosen for myself. It imbues a kind of energy, like warm sunlight shining on me, that is hard to describe, but every bit as real as their food/nutritional benefits.

Sprouts are extremely inexpensive to grow. You can find organic sprouting seeds at most health food stores in the bulk section or you can buy them online at Sunorganic.com. Once you get the process down to a system, it doesn't take much time at all, just a few minutes each day. The benefits are very much worth the effort, as sprouts are without a doubt one of the healthiest foods on the entire planet.

Sprouts are delicious, super nutritious, and a wonderful addition to any meal. Add them to salads, smoothies, soups, eat them plain, top your pate with them, take them in a Ziploc to go for your car, and more! Sprouts are considered a "pre-digested" food, so they are more easily assimilated by your body. It's during the sprouting process that the seeds' protein transforms into amino acids, and the starch converts to simple sugars, making these optimal for digestion. They are a good source of vitamins A, C, E and B-vitamins; hence, they are excellent anti-oxidants. Plus, they contain chlorophyll.

One of my favorites are alfalfa sprouts, which are extremely easy to grow. These sprouts rightly demand great respect, as their roots can extend *100 feet* into the earth to reach minerals and trace elements unreachable by other plant roots. That's bad-ass! I'm also a huge fan of mung sprouts for their thick and crunchy texture, which adds a satisfying fullness to bites. I like adding these to soups and salads for filling and satiating nutrition.

There are two methods from which to choose for your sprouting. I use them both. You can use the old, tested, tried-and-true method of sprouting in glass mason jars, tipped upside down on an angle using a dish drying rack. I love this method (I started with this method) because of the aforementioned reasons about seeing these in your kitchen growing while you tend to them only briefly each day. The other method is to use a machine, such as the Tribest FreshLife Sprouter. I definitely like the FreshLife Sprouter and I do recommend using it. It's easy (so is the jar method though) but the plastic container they grow in is dark, so you can't really see the little guys growing, which is really important to me. So, I do them both. I do the jar method and have 1-3 large jars going at once. Then, so that I can grow even more sprouts to eat, I use the FreshLife Sprouter (*available via links on my Web site, KristensRaw.com/store*).

Another great reason to have both methods going is that while I'm growing wheatgrass with my Freshlife Sprouter, I can grow alfalfa sprouts simultaneously with my glass jars.

HOW TO SPROUT

Directions for the "Jar Method"

You will need several 1/2-gallon and quart size glass mason jars, plus plastic screen lids (available online or at places like Whole Foods' produce section—or just use cheesecloth with a rubber band, but this can get a little messy), a dish drying rack (the folding kind that looks like an X from the side), seeds, and spring water or purified water (tap water will work if necessary, so long as it hasn't been softened/demineralized; do not use distilled water). After soaking and draining off the water, you'll let them sprout in their jars, tipped upside down and setting on an angle on the dish drying rack.

You can use a variety of seeds; start with alfalfa and practice with that. Then, you can start to add other combinations such as clover, onion, broccoli, etc. Use the following:

- 2-3 tablespoons seeds

- Purified, filtered or spring water

Soak the seeds in the water overnight in a half-gallon jar filled with water. The following morning, drain them.

Sprout the seeds for approximately 6 days (tip them upside down and set them on an angle on the dish drying rack), rinsing them and draining them 1-2 times a day (usually only once/day is necessary, but there are times when they might seem dry and a second rinsing and draining might be helpful. Caution here though, if they're too wet, they can get moldy.)

Two days prior to harvesting (about day 4-5), "green" the sprouts by placing them in more light, such as near a window (but avoid direct sunlight).

During these last two days prior to harvest (days 5-6), continue to rinse and drain once or twice a day.

Day 6 or 7, rinse the sprouts in a large bowl of water to loosen their "hulls" (the outer shell of the seeds). Drain off the hulls and water. Put them back into the jar and on the counter for this last day.

Store them in the refrigerator for up to a week in an airtight container or a glass sprouting jar covered with a mesh screen. Continue to rinse and drain every few days until you've gobbled them all up!

Remember, you're starting one jar, but when that jar is done, you'll have to wait another 6-7 days to enjoy sprouts again. For this reason, I recommend always having about three jars going. Start one; then start another, two days later; and then another, two days later; and so on.

If you get mold or your sprouts don't turn out for any other reason, don't worry, just try again. You'll quickly get the hang of it and develop a sense for when to rinse and drain them.

Mung Sprouts

Mung sprouts take less time to sprout. Follow the same instructions as above, using 1/4 cup seeds instead of 2 tablespoons. And, they're ready to eat within 2-3 days. No hulling is needed for these; you can eat them once they have their little sprouted tails. These are an *excellent* source of protein!

CHAPTER 19

WORDS TO INSPIRE

AFFIRMATIONS TO GET YOU STARTED!

As with anything in life, when it comes to adopting the Raw lifestyle, the things you say, think, and focus on will largely determine the extent to which you'll be successful. The following phrases are examples of the kind of thoughts to keep bouncing around in your head. Better yet, say some of them from time to time, or every day, or at every meal... or anytime you need a little encouragement. For extra points, you might even place a few of them on Post-It notes in your kitchen or on your bathroom mirror, where you're sure to see them every day.

- "I am getting stronger and healthier every day because of my new Raw lifestyle!"

- "I am courageous in taking on this new lifestyle!"

- "I love Raw!"

- "Raw is my law!"

- "I am living my ideal life!"

- "This moment is always all I have!"

- "I Rawk!!!"

- "I own my life and I love it!"

- "I love my self!"

- "I'm taking my life to a new level and living it on my terms!"

- "I am mastering my health!"

- "I am creative, loving, and beautiful!"

- "I radiate energy from all of the healthy, fresh Raw food I eat!"

- "I am achieving my goals and it feels wonderful!"

- "I live every day with enthusiasm and power!"

- "I have confidence in my abilities to succeed with Raw and feel better than ever!"

- "I am committed to excellence in everything I do!"

NOW, ON TO YOUR THRILLING JOURNEY!

Thank you so much for taking the time to read this book. I hope it has helped you understand the "why" and "how" of Raw food, as well as motivating you to take this life-changing step into your evolution as the most healthy and beautiful You that you can be!

As always, please send your comments and stories to Kristen@KristensRaw.com.

Printed in the United States
210387BV00004B/14/P